STUDYING The Usual Suspects
Judith Gunn

Contents

Marti
Tel: (

Factsheet

The Usual Suspects

Release Date ....1995, USA
Running Time ....106 mins
Certificate ....R (USA), 18 (UK)
Production Companies ....Polygram Filmed Entertainment, Spelling Films, International, Blue Parrot, Bad Hat Harry Productions, Rosco Film GmbH
Distribution ....Grammercy (theatrical) MGM/UA Home Entertainment (VHS, DVD)

Production Budget

$6 million

Release Dates and Strategies

Premiered at Sundance Film Festival January 1995.
Released weekend of 20 August 1995 on 42 screens (opening weekend gross: $645,363).
US Total Gross: $23,341,568.
UK release 12 September 1995 (total UK box office £2,503,343).

Key Credits

Director ....Bryan Singer

Producers ....Michael McDonnell, Bryan Singer

Screenplay ....Christopher McQuarrie

Director of Photography ....Newton Thomas Siegel

Editor ....John Ottman

Production Designer ....Howard Cummings

Music ....John Ottman

Cast

Stephen Baldwin ....Michael McManus

Gabriel Byrne ....Dean Keaton

Benicio Del Toro ....Fred Fenster

Kevin Pollak ....Todd Hockney

Kevin Spacey ....Roger 'Verbal' Kint

Chazz Palminteri ....Dave Kujan, US Customs

Pete Postlethwaite ....Kobayashi

Giancarlo Esposito ....Jack Baer, FBI

Suzy Amis ....Edie Finneran

Dan Hedaya ....Sgt. Jeffrey 'Jeff' Rabin

Synopsis

This is the story of five guys, one line up and a heist gone wrong. Police and Customs officers try to unravel the means and the motive for the collection of dead men killed in what looks like a gangland fire fight on a boat. They question the one witness who remains alive, Verbal Kint. Verbal tells a story of a line up of five suspects – four professional thieves and a corrupt cop (who was thought to be dead). This combination of criminal minds plans some payback, but they have offended the infamous Keyser Soze and now they owe him…

Introduction

The usual line up

The story of *The Usual Suspects* **(1995) has the kind of 'rags to riches' back story that makes not only the film itself, but the tale of its creation worth telling. This is a study of a film that is not only a ripping yarn but is an exercise in 'virtuoso'[1] directing in the style of film noir. It is an inspiration for students who study media, with its sophisticated dialogue, complex narrative and visual excellence; and an inspiration for students who may have ideas of their own about film-making. Its creation and creators exemplify the difficulties and triumphs of getting a small budget movie made by a set of film-makers who have limited experience but a lot of determination, and an education in film and media. The quality of the film itself and its creation demonstrate that film education and good planning can make a few million dollars go a long way.**

This Guide is intended to support teachers of Media or Film Studies up to A Level. The content of this book can be applied to a variety of areas. Those teaching GCSE can dip into the discussions of narrative (Chapter 3), the film festivals (Chapter 4), the references to film noir as a thriller convention (Chapter 2), pitching and marketing (Chapter 5) and semiotics (Chapter 1).

In general the format of each chapter will begin with a general introduction to relevant theory or discussion and then move towards applying that to the film *The Usual Suspects*. In some chapters, images referred to are listed using the DVD Chapters and Time Code and a brief description. It is therefore possible to target each image discussed on screen exactly. At the end of each chapter there will be Resources for classroom activities associated with that chapter's topic. There will also be a Glossary for the terminology highlighted in bold in each chapter.

Spoiler Warning

In this book we will study a modern classic film, including everything from its inception to its reception but a word of warning – see it before studying it. It has what remains one of the most effective and famous twists in the ending of any film. A twist, of course, is one of the most common conventions of the thriller genre. There is no substitute to seeing this film and experiencing the twist as it was meant to be viewed, so if you have not seen the film read no further. Whether you rent it or buy it – at least see it!

NOTES:

1. Gabriel Byrne, in *Nothing is What it Seems: The Making of The Usual Suspects* (1998).

Semiotics

SEMIOTICS: VISUAL LANGUAGE AND STYLE

In an interview in the TV documentary _Nothing is What it Seems: The Making of The Usual Suspects_ (1998) Gabriel Byrne (Dean Keaton in the film) described _The Usual Suspects_ as a 'brilliant piece of virtuoso directing'. He credits the cinematographer (Newton Thomas Sigel) with making the six million dollar budgeted movie look like it cost a great deal more than that. The film uses visual language with an expertise and confidence not usually expected of such a young director and it is with the study of that visual language that this Guide to _The Usual Suspects_ begins.

In the study of media, the 'text' is any media that is chosen for examination. Students learn to apply their understanding of the word 'text' beyond the idea that a book or a piece of writing is a text. A media text is anything: it is the advertisement in a glossy magazine or is the magazine itself. It is a TV commercial or a radio commercial, it is the news or the movie, it is the computer game or the website. It is true that, in the first instance, a media text can be analysed much like an English text. A media text can be read, viewed or listened to for its meaning. However, aspects of narrative, character and themes can be teased out of even the stillest of images. In the same way, it is the presence of image and audio that makes most media texts different from reading a book. These aspects of audio and image add a further dimension of study and demand additional analysis. It is with images and the semiotics (the language of images) of _The Usual Suspects_ that we shall start.

The makers of the film, including Chris McQuarrie (writer), John Ottman (editor and composer) and Bryan Singer (director), had made an earlier film _Public Access_ (1993) that had been well received by the critics if not by the public. In the course of its release they ran across a magazine article in a New York magazine called 'The Usual Suspects'. It seemed like a good title for a film, so they speculated about a publicity campaign that would be based on the concept of men who were gathered together on suspicion of having committed a crime. They speculated as to the style of image that might accompany the film and thought of the universal image of the identity parade; thus, the poster idea of the line up came into existence. Not long after the showing of their first film, an enquiry was made by a former acquisitions executive turned producer, Robert Jones, as to what their next project would be. This was not an opportunity to be missed so they decided to create a pitch to fit the poster as this image had already focused their intention. Semiotics is the study of images.

From the poster to the last cut, _**The Usual Suspects**_ is an exercise in the use of semiotics, so it's important to gain an understanding of semiotics. It is a study that can underpin the analysis of any media text and is a useful tool for the media student to use.

Semiotics

Semiotics is the language of signs. It is a structural examination of the way in which we understand pictures. One of the originators of the study of images in a structured academic system was Ferdinand de Saussure (1857–1913). Saussure worried about the inadequacy of linguistics. It occurred to him that when one person talks or writes about a dog, the listener or reader visualises the dog in a different way. There is room for miscommunication. Is the dog a Great Dane or a Jack Russell? Without specificity the sender and receiver can be talking about entirely different concepts. Obviously, the use of images provides the sender and the receiver of the language with a more specific concept, a picture that they can both agree on, but Saussure and others, such as C.S. Peirce (1839–1914), soon realised that pictures themselves have hidden or additional meanings that can also be interpreted differently by sender and receiver. These interpretations often depend on the individual's cultural influences. Every image might be transmitted to a receiver with a set of values attached to it; any number of variables might define how both sender and receiver interpret the image.

NOTES:

Saussure came up with the idea of **signifier** + **signified** = *sign*:

Signifier = *dog*.

Signified = *cute look*.

Sign = *a cute dog*.

A 'signifier' is the form which the sign takes.

The 'signified' is the concept it represents.

The 'sign' is the whole that results from the association of the signifier with the signified.

What Saussure recognised in his study of the language of images was that every image came with a significant history, a back story which could be understood by the receiver if he or she had the same cultural references. For example, in Western culture we tend all to understand that the colour black is the colour of mourning. Therefore, the Scottish Widow (Lloyds Bank) advertising image of a hooded widow in a black cape is immediately understood by all who see her as a woman in mourning; but in other cultures the colour of mourning is white. That image, then, would not have the same meaning to a receiver with different cultural references. Semiotics is the understanding and study of the way in which it is the combination of mutual understanding as well as the form itself that give still images their narrative – all students should understand that even a still image has a narrative. Even a cute dog has a narrative. If it is looking up it is asking for love. If it is looking at a biscuit it wants food. A great deal of what governs our understanding of pictures of animals is the way in which we place interpretations on their expressions, interpretations that have much more to do with our understanding of human faces than it does with an actual understanding of animal behaviour.

Tools and Terminology

The media student from GCSE to A level does not have to have an in-depth understanding of the finer points of Saussure's position on semiotics nor even C.S. Peirce's slight variation on the theory (representation, object, interpretant), Lacan's, or anything other than an understanding that images are a language that must be approached with a structured analysis that requires terminology. They need to understand that we all interpret images, and we all understand images both individually and universally. Students must show some evidence of progression from someone who can just observe a picture and understand that it is cute or scary to someone who can understand why some pictures are cute and some are scary.

The idea that a still image has a narrative may be alien to many students, but if they have already understood the concept of connotation then they are on their way to understanding the concept of narrative in a still image. After all 'every picture tells a story', you just have to know how to read it.

The study of images comes with a few tools:

The first two words and methods of analysis that any student must understand are the differences between denotation and connotation. These words have a specific application in the context of Media Studies and, once mastered, they are a demonstration of a student's understanding of the task of analysis and they make that task more effective. Let's go back to the picture of the dog.

Denotation is simply the description of what is placed in the picture. This picture denotes a dog, a small dog looking up. The dog is mainly black with tan eyebrows. The picture is a close up on the dog's face. The dog's ears are flopped forward.

NOTES:

Semiotics

His eyes are open and he is looking straight at the viewer. That is what the picture denotes. Denotation is a description of the signifier.

Connotation, like it or not, requires interpretation, which only works (as we have seen) if we all have the same cultural influences, but in this case the influences are likely to be universal. The picture denotes a dog looking up and this connotes its vulnerability. Children look up to parents (physically, that is); it is therefore a universal indicator of vulnerability on the part of the one looking up and responsibility on the part of the one looking down. From this connotation we can further suggest that the dog is cute because we are programmed (most of us) to see the vulnerable as cute, in order that we don't reject the young, and thereby jeopardise the future of the whole human race.

Denotation and connotation together point to the **sign**, the complete picture as it is intended to be portrayed. Some images, however, go beyond their intention: connotations can be symbolic or iconic.

Iconic is another term where the language of images requires the student to be specific. We have cultural icons such as Princess Diana and Marilyn Monroe. They are icons in the sense that their existence and position in society, as well as their look, represent certain aspects of the culture to the viewer. In both cases ideas of beauty are affirmed, but also lifestyles. In Princess Diana's case, ideas of royalty, romance and charity are associated with her, as well as British nationalistic issues. In Marilyn Monroe's case, the American Dream and the hidden flawed nature of that dream are associated with her, as well as nostalgia for a bygone age. However, an image that is an icon in semiotics remains an object that bears some resemblance to that which it is representing. Hence, religious icons depict Madonna and child or Christ in a recognisable and concrete form. Icons in this sense are like logos, single images that represent something, anything from the icons in Windows software to road signs.

A symbol is a sign that we recognise because we have agreed to recognise it as such; that is, by convention. The Union Jack is accepted as the British flag because society has agreed that it will be the British flag. These are signs governed by culture, but not all of them are as obvious as a flag, the skull and crossbones or the Christian symbol of the cross.

A **referent** is a useful and easy bit of terminology when analysing pictures. It is also a neat little trick for designers. This is when the sign or picture refers to something else; it reminds you of something else. An obvious example is the 'T' in the credits logo of *The Vicar of Dibley* – the 'T' has a referent – it's the Christian cross. In that case the referent is clearly recognisable, but when lettering resembles a face in the sand, for instance, in the poster of the film ***The Mummy*** (1999, dir. Stephen Sommers), then the referent is slightly more subtle.

An **indexical image** is another simple concept in the world of semiotic analysis. It is an image that indexes either scale or the passing of time. A good example is the scene from ***Jaws*** (1975, dir. Steven Spielberg) just after the principal characters have seen the shark for the first time. The character Matt (Richard Dreyfuss), tries to persuade his colleague Police Chief Brody (Roy Scheider) to step out on the farthest part of the prow of the boat so that he can take a photograph. When Chief Brody, under protest, asks why, the reply is 'I need something for scale!' Thus, Chief Brody is an indexical image that could also be supper. More often indexical images demonstrate the passing of time, the clock hands dissolving forward. A series of newspapers spinning towards

NOTES:

the screen, the number of cigarettes in the ash tray or at the character's feet, the number of cups of coffee drunk: these are all short cuts to telling the audience that time has passed, without having to go to the effort of using the time to show it.

Polysemic images offer another opportunity for interpretation, in fact, that is precisely what they do: a polysemic image is one that can be open to several interpretations. These images can be governed by our own cultural understanding. A rose, for instance, can have several meanings. It has associations with love and sex. A bunch of roses is reputedly sent to a lady after she has consummated her relationship with her suitor, but the rose has thorns. Roses are stunningly beautiful to look at and to smell but they can be mean when you pick them up. A picture of a rose is a truly polysemic image. It denotes a beautiful flower, it connotes an association with sex and love (particularly if the colour is red); but it also connotes a hidden danger, a hidden capacity to hurt. The red rose's connotations are many; hence, it is a polysemic image.

Perhaps one of the most famous polysemic images is the crown of thorns. Its referent is a crown or, in the context of its time, a crown of laurel leaves that carried with it the connotations of divinity and victory. The thorns connote the fact that those who crowned Jesus did not recognise his claims. To Christians the thorns connote the blood and the suffering that this son of God went through for them. To contemporise the image, it is an icon of the message of Christianity and to some extent the Western culture that rests upon it.

NOTES:

Semiotics and The Suspects

An understanding of semiotics, the ability to use the word and know what it means and to use the terminology toolbox, is a strong basis on which to place a study not only of the film *The Usual Suspects*, but of any media text. The reason for this relevance to a study of *The Usual Suspects* is because the film itself is a visual exercise in polysemic meanings. It tells one story whilst quite definitely telling another at the same time. If you view the film twice you get an entirely different story the second time round: the same images tell a different story. Before we begin with the moving images we will examine its most famous still image. What narrative does this image offer?

In fact the poster has a variety of incarnations but the earliest one ran the picture with the advertising tag line 'Five Criminals, One line up. No Coincidence'. See the following:

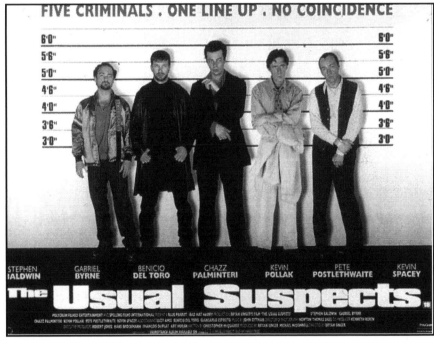

Semiotics

In fact there are a huge number of variations on this poster. An exercise at the end of this chapter is to compare some of them and see what differences there are and suggest reasons as to why they differ.

What does it denote?

- Five men against a height chart.
- The horizontal lines of the chart run behind the men.
- The men are grouped together staring at the camera.
- They are not smiling.
- The tallest man is in the centre.
- When seen in colour, the man to the left of him is wearing a cream suit.
- The man in the cream suit has his jacket over his arm. He is slightly side-on to the camera.
- The man on the right of him is holding his own arm.
- The tallest man in the centre is wearing a black suit and a red shirt.
- The man on the left side of the centre is all in black.
- The man on the far left is slouching slightly and is wearing red on top with black trousers.
- The picture is slightly over-exposed – very light.
- The tag line is at the top and in red capitals.
- The title is in reversed out white type at the bottom.
- All the type is reversed out of a black background except the age certification.

Having offered our denotations, our connotations are as follows:

- When seen in colour, the man wearing white or cream has the connotations of a hero, a good protagonist.
- This man also has a slightly defiant stance. His hand is on his hip. His expression is angry.
- The man wearing black has the connotations of an antagonist.
- The men wearing red are signifying danger.
- The man holding his arm looks weak and vulnerable.
- The type is in red above them, also signifying danger.
- The reversed out type is very stark and white. It looks a bit like a stamp – its referent is a stamp and in later versions of the poster and on the DVD this referent is clearly used.
- The over-exposed light signifies a photograph, as if it is in the act of being taken.
- The signified is five men in a line up; the signifier is the context and the expression on their faces. The connotations of both are that they are five criminals, but, culturally, we know that in a line up, only one man is guilty and the question is, which one is it?

The primary purpose of the poster (of any poster in fact) is to draw attention to the object. In this case the object is the film and the poster is intended to advertise not only the existence of the film, but its genre. The poster does this by employing the semiotic codes that point to the generic conventions of the genre. The language of images acts as a subconscious code that begins to tell us what to expect. While the film itself may use obscurity and mystery to aid the telling of its story, ultimately the advertising campaign must indicate to the audience some hint of what to expect. Thus, while the semiotic codes indicate some aspects of the story, most importantly they point to the genre.

Mise-en-scène

The background against which the men are taken is the police height chart. The height chart is, of course, an iconic image. It may not be a universal image but it is certainly widely understood by its audience. It has connotations of police involvement, crime, guilt and innocence, mystery and resolution.

The poster cannot be argued to be the reason for the success of the film, but it certainly did an effective job in drawing attention to the film. The success of the film in the end depended on the strength of the script and its performances, but so successful did they both become that the

NOTES:

An earlier line up: *The Asphalt Jungle*

phrase (known in English as a lexical set) and the poster became a cliché. The poster has been mimicked by any number of other ensemble groups, everyone from **Friends** to **The Simpsons** have lined up before that height chart.

The poster is also an intertextual reference. An intertextual reference is a reference by one text to another. It can be as direct as verbal reference; for example, as the young people in the film **Wrong Turn** (2003, dir. Rob Schmidt) approach a ramshackle cabin in the middle of West Virginia one of the characters reminds them of the existence of the movie **Deliverance** (1972, dir. John Boorman), although such references are usually more subtle. In fact the name of Bryan Singer's company Bad Hat Harry Productions is an intertextual reference itself: it is a quote from **Jaws**.

Semiotics or the language of images is as difficult to quantify as the success of a best seller or the rise of fame of a hitherto unknown actor or film. If agents and producers could identify what makes the syntax of film work they would copy it, which, of course, is what they do and that's what makes a genre.

The poster for **The Usual Suspects** does have a predecessor and that predecessor, in itself, gives an indicator to both the genre and style of the movie. One of the abiding images from the film **The Asphalt Jungle** (1950) is that of a line up. A

film noir directed by John Huston, **The Asphalt Jungle** is heralded as a naturalistic film noir, a real clue as to the genre of **The Usual Suspects**.

Codes

Codes are different from conventions and in the case of **The Usual Suspects** this is important to recognise. Codes once again refer to the semiotics of the moving image and to the use of audio or certain repeated techniques and devices that speak the language of the particular genre. **The Usual Suspects** is often referred to as a 'neo noir', a film noir for the nineties (see Chapter 2). Film noir is a style, rather than a genre in itself, but its visual codes tend to be associated with the genre conventions of thriller. They depict dark goings on in dark places and act as a metaphor for the human mind and heart at their most devious.

Codes include the following:

- The use of light and shadow.

- The use of camera angles.

- The use of colour and clothing.

- The use of sound.

The kinds of codes used in a film are directly linked to the genre of that film. In a Western, for instance, codes include guns, horses, spurs, saloon doors, huge locations and spectacular light, small people and their deeds set against a

NOTES:

huge sky. Science fiction includes codes of technologically advanced worlds or futures – anything from hover skate boards to a world run by machines.

As genres become tired and the audience gets bored with the same old saloon doors and gunfights, the codes of other conventions can be employed to change the atmosphere and connotation of a well-tried genre. In *Unforgiven* (1992), director Clint Eastwood employs the big sky, the huge location and the cowboy music; but in its darkest moments *Unforgiven* uses the codes of film noir, perhaps because it has become recognised that film noir is a universal semiotic language for the connotations attached to desperate deeds.

The use of the codes and conventions of film noir style are prevalent in *The Usual Suspects* which is why it has been given the epithet of a 'Neo noir'. In the Chapter 2 we shall look in more detail at the visual style and antecedents of the codes and conventions of *The Usual Suspects*.

SEMIOTICS OF SCENES – THE USUAL SUSPECTS

The Semiotics of Colour
The colour red is a significant colour in our culture: it is the colour of blood, it signifies danger and it signifies passion. In *The Usual Suspects* red is the basic code of blood and danger, and each suspect has a red moment.

Fenster
The most obvious use of red is the red shirt that Fenster wears in the beginning and Fenster is the first to die. He is wearing it when he is picked up. He is wearing black, another colour signifier, when he is found dead.

Hockney
At the introduction of Todd Hockney, a close up on him shows him wiping his face with a red handkerchief (DVD Chapter 3: Time Code 00:05:45).

McManus
McManus has a red leather jacket that he wears when he commits his most violent act, the killing of Saul Berg's bodyguards in the job commissioned by Redfoot (DVD Chapter 17: Time Code 00:44:32).

Dean Keaton
Keaton wears a red shirt as the doom deepens in the billiard room and the suspects are confronted by Mr Kobayashi (DVD Chapter 21: Time Code 00:49:50).

He wears a red cravat during the heist commissioned by Redfoot (DVD Chapter 16: Time Code 00:45:05).

At the end of film during Dave Kujan's narrative Keaton's face is lit in red to imply Kujan's interpretation of him as the villain, perhaps even the devil (DVD Chapter 30: Time Code 01:29:55).

Verbal Kint
Verbal never wears anything bright red although his patterned shirts hint at it.

The use of colour throughout the film is carefully employed. The curtains that the suspects stand next to when Mr Kobayashi shows them Edie Finneran are red. The walls in the billiard room are ochre.

Black and White
In the first scene when Dean Keaton is picked up he is wearing a cream suit; he has the semiotics of the good man. As such, he signifies that he is the protagonist, the white knight. Kobayashi is always in a dark suit.

Verbal Kint is in black throughout the interrogation and it is clear when he leaves the police station. His colours are the binary opposite of Keaton's.

Pick almost any moment from the interrogation and you will see that Verbal Kint is filmed from a high angle: he is seated, often looking up – vulnerable.

NOTES:

He often looks small; the semiotics of the interrogation room are entirely designed to fool us into viewing Kint as weak and harmless. Just occasionally Spacey's performance hints otherwise: have a look at DVD Chapter 15: Time Code 00:40:15. (He did know the ending when he played the part.)

Verbal thinks things through

The Usual Suspects is so packed with visual content and semiotics that it is difficult to stop analysing. At the end, McManus darts across the roof in front of a full moon, as he hunts through the ship; the chaos of their cause is juxtaposed by McManus finding a quiet if nervous Alsatian on the boat. Symbols and imagery abound. Perhaps not all the semiotics were intended, but Kevin Spacey says of Bryan Singer[2] that he knew exactly what he wanted. He was not a director who threw everything together in the hope of sorting it out in editing. He knew what shots he wanted, he planned and executed them, exactly as he visualised the film. That takes detailed storyboards, careful scripting, and forethought on lighting, angles and props. Media students should employ a little of that practice in their own work.

Total Trivia

When Keaton opens the briefcase and hands out the envelopes given to him by Mr Kobayashi, he hands them out in the order in which the characters die.

Table 1.1 The Semiotics of Angles

Image	Angle
DVD Chapter 3: Time Code 00:04:59. Verbal's introduction.	When we first meet Verbal he is giving testimony. There is a bright light trained on his head that picks out his face like a skull. His face is framed by the court coat of arms that grows out of his head like horns; the symbols of good and evil are behind him. His **referent** is the horned beast.
DVD Chapter 3: Time Code 00:06:20. Kujan's introduction.	When we first meet Dave Kujan he is filmed from a low angle coming down the stairs. He and his colleagues look powerful. When he speaks to Keaton in the scene, a point of view (POV) shot from the table makes Kujan look powerful.
DVD Chapter 3: Time Code 00:07:08. Keaton's arrest.	As they arrest Keaton a rat-in-the trap shot is used (high angle down on the table). Keaton is a white rat surrounded by darkness, he has nowhere to run.
DVD Chapter 11: Time Code 00:28:50.	When Keaton and Kint confront each other later they do so in Keaton's hi tech minimalist flat; the two men are alienated and small in the sterile surroundings. The pair look unnatural in the bright light, against white walls; darkness is their habitat.
DVD Chapter 14: Time Code 00:35:58.	This is an extreme close up (ECU) of Kujan and a background mid shot of Rabin in deep focus and close up, it is a classic film noir shot of the sleuths, confused but dedicated. They are dressed in black and white; the contrast emphasises the dilemma that they face. More of film noir in Chapter 2.
DVD Chapter 18: Time Code 00:46:58.	At the confrontation between Redfoot and the suspects at the Korean Friendship Bell, the opening shot is a low angle shot on Verbal; it is one of the few times he looks powerful. The low angle continues as the men argue; this is a titanic struggle. When the confrontation ends the men draw their guns; again, there is a worm's eye view on the outstretched arms and guns. This is a classic Western convention, a reference, even down to the cowboy hat that one of them wears.

NOTES:

2. *Nothing Is What It Seems: The Making of The Usual Suspects* (1998).

Classroom Worksheets

Semiotics

Take the following picture and adapt it in any way to tell a story. You could do this by ripping the picture up and sticking it back together in a fragmented way. You could use colour, trace out silhouettes from the picture and rearrange. You could add text that indicates that it is attached to a certain genre. Use your imagination.

The Usual Message?

See how many versions of the poster for **The Usual Suspects** you can find – 'Images' on Google is a good place to start, and a few are shown below. You might think that there has only been one version of the poster – think again. Spot the differences between them and try to establish why different versions have been published. Answer the questions below.

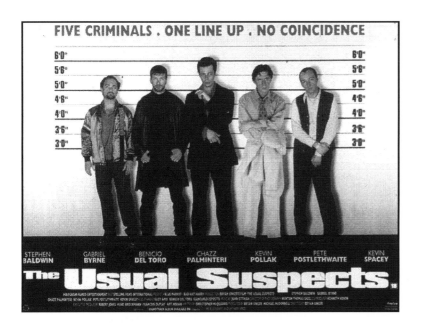

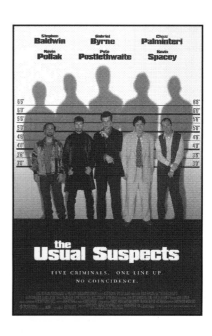

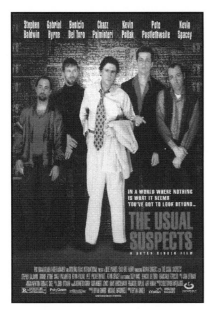

- What does each poster **denote** and **connote**?

- Why does the central character change?

- What colour differences are there?

- Why do the colours change?

Write a few sentences, using correct terminology, on the nature of these posters.

Stars and Casting

Pick at least two of your favourite Hollywood stars and see if you can track back their career through their biography or filmography.

- Where did they start?

- Was it as part of an ensemble cast?

See which proportion of movie stars started in an ensemble film of whatever genre. If your favourite stars did not start that way, see if you can identify a genre of style in your taste in films.

- Are you a fan of the Hollywood mainstream or a bit alternative in your taste?

Mise-en-scène

Choose a particular scene from **The Usual Suspects** and analyse the mise-en-scène. Look for the following:

- Use of light.

- Use of colour in clothing.

- The way props and furniture are placed on the set.

- The placing of the characters in the scene.

The following are a few examples:

- In the interview room, how does the set reflect the fact that they are in a police station?

- In the snooker hall, how is colour and position used to juxtapose the feeling of threat against the idea of friendship and bonding between the men? Think where else you might have seen the snooker scene.*

TASK

Either:

- Design in detail a floor plan and light design for the interrogation scene. Discuss how the light, position and angle of the police and suspect define and represent the characters.

and/or:

- Use a digital camera and as much lighting technique as you can to imitate the interrogation scenes and offer an analysis of character and representation.

*Teacher's note: The snooker hall is seen on the top of the cigar box in the office.

Classroom Worksheets

CHAPTER 1 GLOSSARY: TEACHER COPY

Term	Definition
Cinematographer	The member of the crew who is in charge of the photography on the set. This means shooting the movie and supplying the technical ability for the Director to get the shot with the colour, light and angle that he/she wants.
Pitch	The process by which a prospective film-maker offers ideas to those who have the money and the power to commission the film.
Semiotics	The study of the language of signs (images).
Signifier	The object in the picture.
Signified	The implications (such as expression) of that object in the picture.
Sign	The combination of the sign and the signified that make the picture.
Denotation	The process of describing what is actually in the picture.
Connotation	The process of describing the meanings, such as cultural references, attached to a picture or an image.
Iconic	The use of an image as a representation.
Symbol	Something that represents something else by association; for example, the Christian cross, the yin yang image.
Referent	The use of an object in graphic representations so that the image refers to the object – e.g logos for *The Vicar of Dibley*, *The Sopranos*.
Indexical image	An image that narrates a story, such as the passing of time – ticking clock.
Polysemic	Several meanings contained in a picture – e.g. a rose.
Mise-en-scène	What is placed on and used in the set.
Intertextual	The way in which texts will reference each other – the 'Battle of the Banjos' music from **Deliverance** has become one of the most famous and often used intertextual references.
Conventions	The formulas of narrative and iconography that repeat themselves in films.
Ensemble	A group or team of people that work together on the same project.
Heist	To hold up or rob.
Codes	The visual clues which are also formulaic in identifying genre.
Low angle	The camera films from a low angle looking up.
High angle	The camera films from a high angle looking down.
Point of view (POV)	The camera takes the point of view of a character.
Worm's eye view	The camera films from a very low angle as if it were a worm looking up.
Extreme close up (ECU)	The camera is so close to the subject that they fill the screen (usually faces).
Close up	The camera focuses on the character or subject as a large part of the composition.
Deep focus	When everything in the shot is in focus and the characters usually face the camera and not each other.
Rat-in-the-trap	A high angle shot that makes a character look trapped.
Storyboards	A pictorial plan of a film.

CHAPTER 1 GLOSSARY: STUDENT COPY

Term	Definition
Cinematographer	The member of the crew who is in charge of the photography on the set. This means shooting the movie and supplying the technical ability for the Director to get the shot with the colour, light and angle that he/she wants.
Pitch	The process by which a prospective film-maker offers ideas to those who have the money and the power to commission the film.
Semiotics	
Signifier	
Signified	
Sign	
Denotation	
Connotation	
Iconic	
Symbol	
Referent	
Indexical image	
Polysemic	
Mise-en-scène	
Intertextual	
Conventions	
Ensemble	
Heist	
Codes	
Low angle	
High angle	
Point of view (POV)	
Worm's eye view	
Extreme close up (ECU)	
Close up	
Deep focus	
Rat-in-the-trap	
Storyboards	

The Usual Suspects as Neo Noir

In Chapter 1 we explored semiotics as the study of representation through the language of images, but representation in film is much more than that. If it were not, then our study would only be the study of the still image. Representation in film includes movement, sound and story and, like semiotics, representation includes interaction; that which is communicated interacts with those to whom it communicates.

Representation

Representation is precisely what it says it is – it is the 're' presentation of something we already know and understand. The process of representation requires 'recognition', the fact that we already know the subject that is being represented. If we want to represent fear to an audience, that audience needs to be able to recognise aspects of the representation. A look of terror, a wide-eyed scream, a narrative that involves peril, both Janet Leigh and daughter Jamie Leigh-Curtis have had their screen scream moments. Janet Leigh was Hitchcock's shower girl in *Psycho* (1960). She is blonde and beautiful and not a very good girl and she dies in the shower, stabbed to death. Her screaming represents her fear and pain, her blank expression as she slides down the wall, her imminent death. Daughter Jamie Leigh survives her ordeal in *Halloween* (1978, dir. John Carpenter) but only after a deal of screaming trapped in a wardrobe. Both women represented victims; both narratives involve a psycho and murder.

The two murderous representations denote many of the same elements: a young woman, screaming, a lot of stabbing and a murderer. The connotations of the representations are slightly different. The woman does fight back in the later film and representations of women in film as a whole have moved on from the helpless screamer to the dangerous female (or the 'final girl' in slasher films). There are always exceptions, of course, as there are in life but what remains true, in general, is the youth and beauty of the woman in peril.

Representation, then, has a context: the ideology of the community of viewers needs to be content that the representations they are being offered are recognisable and, increasingly, women in the audience no longer recognise themselves as helpless victims of random violence. They are inclined to an ideology that demands they fight back and that has been represented recently through everything from Ripley (*Alien*, 1979, dir. Ridley Scott) to Buffy (*Buffy The Vampire Slayer*, TV Series 1997, w. Joss Whedon).

Representation, then, conforms to the presentations we have in society and there is a controlling ideology, or **hegemony** (dominant ideology), defining the structure of our society: this may range from having to wear school uniform, getting money by having a job, having children, taking a holiday at Christmas, to visiting the family. These are all part of Western culture's controlling ideas and most films work with that ideology even if they challenge it. For example, most black actors will state that acting in the 1970s for them consisted of taking roles that represented their community as criminal; the controlling idea defined a stereotype, detrimental to that community. Directors such as Spike Lee and actors as far back as Sidney Poitier challenged those dominant ideas.[3]

The need for a context for representation is partly what governs genre. Genre defines the type of representation the audience is likely to get. It tells the audience that they will see crime representations or comedy representations: genre defines the context and narrows down the controlling ideology.

Genre

Genre is the concept of similar but different. In terms of images, it might very well be seen as art in a certain 'school', but this is the study of the moving image; not only does it look similar – although sometimes it may not even do that – but genre will tell a similar story in a similar way.

The principle of genre for all students to understand from GCSE onwards is that it is largely based on the principle of making money. Stories of the same type offer the audience and

---

NOTES:

3. Amongst Spike Lee's early films *She's Gotta Have It* (1986) portrayed a middle class black America preoccupied with sex and money just like any other colour. Sidney Poitier's early work including *A Raisin in the Sun* (1961, dir. Daniel Petrie), *The Bedford Incident* (1965, dir. James B. Harris) and *In the Heat of the Night* (1967, dir. Norman Jewison) represented black people in roles other than those associated with crime.

the producer/exhibitor security. The problem with genre is that the audience can tire of it, and a genre that stops making money no longer gets made. This may disappoint some but it may also inspire change and adaptations. *The Usual Suspects* is a heist movie, using an ensemble cast. The simple definition of the genre to which *The Usual Suspects* conforms is that of a thriller and, because it involves robbery rather than serial killing, it is in the sub-genre of heist.

Conventions

What defines a genre are the conventions it uses. These are the common elements of narrative and characterisation.

The language of the media is rarely difficult – there is little French, and (I think) no Latin. The word 'thriller' means what it says: it describes a story that thrills. In early interviews with Huw Wheldon[4] (*Monitor: Hitchcock on Hitchcock* – BBC Archive programme, ed. Nick Freand Jones, 1997) Hitchcock describes thrillers as 'switchback' rides. Good thrillers are like a ride on a rollercoaster: fear, excitement and relief. The definition of a 'thriller' is precisely that, a rollercoaster ride of thrills and excitement. What define any genre are the conventions that it uses. In the case of a thriller they are as follows:

Narrative

- Crime – crime is defined differently by different societies. It is in fact the failure by the characters to conform to the hegemony.

- Murder – the oldest crime in the book and the greatest injustice in life and one that the societal consensus rarely disagrees on – the taking of a life.

- Mystery – the question: if not *who* did it, then *why* did they do it?

- The creation of suspense and tension – often related to the attempts to solve the crime.

- Deception – sometimes this deception is played on the audience, sometimes the audiences see it played out amongst the characters.

- Surprise – the attempt to delight with a thrill, a shiver of fear or an unexpected event.

- Twist – the ultimate unexpected event, the one that explains everything.

Both narrative and character are discussed in more detail in Chapter 3 but we will visit character briefly here, as it relates more specifically to this discussion of film noir style.

Characters

- Victim – as we see in the examples of both Janet and Jamie Leigh, the victim is often a woman, but nearly all thriller genre texts deal with the attempt to solve an injustice. The most common convention is the murder of a woman, it fits the controlling ideology – in fact most victims of random violence are young men.

- Protagonist – not be confused with the hero. This is the character (more commonly now female) whose story we follow as they attempt to solve the problem or become more embedded in it. Just occasionally the protagonist is also the antagonist.

- Antagonist – this is the character who is the opposition in the film, again male or female; they are judged by the consensus to be wrong.

- Femme fatale – almost the exact opposite of the woman as victim, this woman is more likely to make the man the victim; she may often be the catalyst for crime.

Film Noir

As we will see in Chapter 6 on auteur theory the preoccupation of cinematic representation in the early days was to re-present stories on film as closely as possible to their original representation. As the art of cinema developed, representations began to include conscious reference to connotations, and ideas of semiotics, symbolism and signification began to be represented on screen. The genre of the crime thriller leant itself to a certain style of filming that the French community of critics, newly exposed to a deluge of Hollywood film post-world war two, labelled film noir.

NOTES:

4. *Monitor*, BBC 1962, http://www.hitchcock.nl/quo.htm; also *Close Up On Hitchcock*, BBC 1997, Prod. Nick Freand Jones.

The Usual Suspects as Neo Noir

Metropolis, top, and *Nosferatu*, above: early expressionist influences on noir

Film noir is not a genre. This can be confusing for the novice student: film noir is not merely defined by mise-en-scène, storyline, character or story formula but is more defined by its mood, tone and style. Thus, it is possible to have a science fiction film noir (***Blade Runner***, 1982, dir. Ridley Scott) or a Western film noir (***Unforgiven***). It might be frustrating for students who, having just got the idea of what genre is and how to identify it, are now told that film noir might be something that has common elements, but that, in itself, is not a genre. Noir style acts like a painting style that affects both the narrative and the visual impact of the film. German expressionists painted pictures of landscapes and of people in similar styles; noir is a film director's paint on narrative and vision. Fritz Lang's ***Metropolis*** (1927) employed the expressionist vision while ***Nosferatu*** (1922, dir. F.W. Murnau) developed the chiaroscuro lighting, all sources for the vision of noir.

The visual style of noir was not only made possible by the inspiration of German expressionism but by technological progress in terms of cameras and lighting. Cameras became more portable and able to work with minimal light. It became possible to paint with light; to use shadow, silhouette and high contrast. Visual signifiers became part of the semiotics of noir: characters' faces were half lit, part in shadow part in bright light. They signified the duality of the stories and the characters themselves. Scenes were played out in rooms striped by the shadows of bars, but which were, in fact, Venetian blinds. Faces stepped into the light, shadows moved across the set, tortured characters faced the camera all in stark focus (a technique known as deep focus that had recently become possible). Characters climbed spiral staircases or clattered chaotically down them into their own personal hell. Dingy street lights half revealed the activities of fugitives or strangers and when revelation did come, light was often used to pinpoint the culprit both literally and symbolically, as, at the end of ***The Big Combo*** (1955, dir. Joseph H. Lewis), when the female protagonist traps her attacker for the police in a car spotlight against

the wall. He cannot escape from the light of revelation or capture.

The first film to be identified as a film noir was ***Stranger on the Third Floor*** (1940, dir. Boris Ingster) about a young reporter who witnesses a murder. While world war two raged, Hollywood tried to stoke morale by offering the audience musicals and romantic comedies. Another contender for first noir a year later was ***The Maltese Falcon*** (1941, dir. John Huston). This story contained all the ingredients of the typical noir – a private eye seduced into an investigation by a woman, who is not what she claimed to be, all based on a novel by Dashiel Hammett. The hard boiled detective novel, the pulp fiction of its day, was plundered for its noir stories: Hammett, Raymond Chandler (***The Big Sleep***), James M. Cain (***The Postman Always Rings Twice***) provided dangerous femmes fatale, cool private eyes and middle class victims. Storyline did not define noir as a genre but it did demonstrate some common conventions. Noir dealt with ordinary men, apparently good, often middle class, but who could be corrupted by greed and sex. At first their stories seem unrelated to world events, but in the end the central characters were good men gone wrong, people lured into worlds of crime and misdeeds. These characters were innocents in a chaotic universe, just like soldiers at war.

Film noir, however, took the human psyche in a different direction. These men were not heroes in battle, but neither were they arch criminals; they were not men who wanted to participate in crime and chaos, but men who could be tempted to cross the line. They were men who were not quite able to reject the attractions of money, sex and a better life. Perhaps the classic example of this kind of early noir film is ***Double Indemnity*** (1944, dir. Billy Wilder).

The film starts by depicting a dying, already repentant Walter Neff (Fred MacMurray) confessing to a murder he committed, one he executed at the behest of a devastating blonde Phyllis Dietrichson (played by Barbara Stanwyck) for insurance fraud.

NOTES:

Love and murder at first sight: *Double Indemnity*

Double Indemnity uses many of the classic conventions and codes of a film noir, not least the stunning blonde, whose representation Wilder began to regret even as they were filming. The wig was too thick and too *blonde*, a cliché of the blonde who has more fun variety, but four weeks into filming it was too late to change it. He justified it by suggesting that the exaggerated representation was intended.[5] Other aspects of the film used subtler semiotics in that the early scenes are shot in the bright light of a California summer and as the story deepens, the location is the night, the light minimalist and dark, and it is at night that the confession is made.

Perhaps one of the bleakest representations of film noir is the film ***Detour*** (1945, dir. Edgar G. Ulmer). A young man literally takes a detour when the man he has hitched a ride with dies and the protagonist descends into a worsening spiral of blackmail, wrong turns and murder. The end is ambiguous but the controlling ideology of the time could not quite countenance the idea of the escape of the criminal – crime must be punished. The first flush of noir ended in 1958 – many cite the strange nuclear noir ***Kiss Me Deadly*** (dir. Robert Aldrich based on the novel by Micky Spillane) as the final noir of that period. The intervention of the nuclear age and the cold war began to change the context in which noir was created and other genres, such as the arrival of the kitchen sink drama and its angry young men, began to reflect different representations in cinema. The final swan song of post-war noir is Orson Welles' ***Touch of Evil*** (1958) (a pre-***Psycho*** movie for Janet Leigh). Welles depicts a world of gangsters, racketeers and a cruelly corrupt cop, played by Welles himself, grotesquely disfigured by corpulent expressionist make-up. It closed the world of noir, at least for a while.

NOTES:

5. Taken from an interview conducted in 1975 and published in *Film Noir Reader 3*, edited by Robert Porfirio, Alain Silver and James Ursini (2001). Excerpt reproduced in www.imagesjournal.com.

The Usual Suspects as Neo Noir

Neo Noir

Devotees of film noir will not credit that a film made after the 1950s can be called a true film noir. The date, the colour and the political circumstances militate against it. Noir, say the purists, is a style of film that is tied to its time, nothing that came after can truly be called a noir. However, this would be to deny a body of work that follows in the style of noir. William Hurt and Kathleen Turner's passionate *Body Heat*, (1981, dir. Lawrence Kasdan) made no attempt to hide its noir roots (it's virtually a remake of of *Double Indemnity*), while actual remakes such as *The Postman Always Rings Twice* (1981, dir. Bob Rafelson) and original films such as *Se7en* (1995, dir. David Fincher) have plunged the audience into a darkness both narrative and visual.

Bryan Singer's production career was that of a student amateur while at USC, but any study of film history would address the presence of noir, analyse its codes, conventions and style. It is worth noting that Bryan Singer studied Film History at The University of Southern California (USC School of Cinema–Television). He made films in his spare time, a fact for all young aspiring media makers to note. (Students are unlikely to succeed in the media if they only meet the minimum requirements for the job.) A familiar style was a good start for a young director to expand upon in his second film. Gabriel Byrne (Dean Keaton) does state that every bit of technique that Singer knew was brought to play in his filming of *The Usual Suspects*[6]– so is *The Usual Suspects* a Neo Noir?

Noir Conventions

This analysis fundamentally demonstrates the use of noir techniques in *The Usual Suspects*. Its narrative reflects the classic twists and turns of a noir thriller. Most particularly one man, Dean Keaton, descends into a spiral of doom, just as in *Detour*, often cited as one of the darkest films noirs ever made.[7] Once a character embarks on a certain course, he is fated never to redeem himself (and it is often a man). In Keaton's case the story of his downfall starts before *The Usual Suspects* begins. According to the story he has been a

corrupt and vicious cop; the film begins three years after he has left all that behind and he is trying to set up a legitimate business, but he cannot escape his past and everything he does to finish it simply leads him deeper into disaster and ultimately death.

The Blonde
(Femme Fatale or Victim?)

The Usual Suspects lacks a femme fatale; there is a blonde, Edie Finneran (played by Suzy Amis) and she may or may not be implicated in the crime story, but she is not the temptress. Throughout the movie she appears only briefly and her role is largely as the damsel in distress. She is tossed about by the events and then discarded. *The Usual Suspects* is a very male film. The film's narrative, its characters (to a certain extent), even its love interest (between McManus and Fenster) are all male dominated.

The Protagonist

The discussion of narrative in this book will indicate that the identification of the protagonist in *The Usual Suspects* is not easy to identify, just as there is no easily identifiable femme fatale. Candidates for the protagonist hover between the central narrative and, therefore, Verbal Kint, who tells the story of Dean Keaton and his attempt to go straight, despite the spiral of fate and temptation that pulls him down and Dave Kujan who is the sleuth. Each of these characters carries the stamp of noir which adds to the atmosphere of the *The Usual Suspects* as a noir style film.

The Antagonist

The Usual Suspects is played out on a large scale. A group of men are tempted into a spiral that leads to the death of them all and many others besides. The kind of violence portrayed at the end of the film would merit a fair bit of live coverage on CNN. *The Usual Suspects* has a serious antagonist; it is not a selfish woman who wants her husband's life insurance, not a lover who wants to possess that which he cannot have and will do anything to get it. *The Usual Suspects* has an antagonist to beat all antagonists. He is a comic book bad guy, a James Bond villain. There is even some suggestion that he is the Devil himself:

NOTES:

6. *Nothing is What It Seems: The Making of The Usual Suspects*, 1998.
7. Weston, R., 'Detour' (1945), www.filmonthly.com/Noir/Articles/Detour/html.

Keyser Soze is the stuff of nightmares, an evil genius who lacks empathy even for his wife and children, a man who can perpetuate a myth about himself that terrifies even the toughest of criminals. A man who will do what the other guy won't.

It is the antagonist in *The Usual Suspects* who gives it some of that neo noir edge. The antagonist (if he exists) is a little bit melodramatic. His name strikes fear into all who hear it. He has a murderous back story (as a man who killed his own family). He is a man that the only living witness calls the Devil.

'The greatest trick the Devil ever pulled was convincing the world he did not exist' (Verbal Kint referring to Keyser Soze in interrogation). In addition Verbal Kint, who is the likeliest contender for the title of Keyser Soze (if he exists at all), appears to have a club foot, an ancient sign of the Devil and a cloven fist also an ancient sign of the Devil. The possibility of the supernatural is what makes *The Usual Suspects* just that little bit more compelling, but monsters and myths, and the cynicism of noir are not comfortable bed fellows.

Ensemble

Among the conventions that *The Usual Suspects* uses is that of the ensemble cast. Typically, of course, the ensemble cast is not a unique convention to thriller. Romantic comedies, Westerns, sci-fi and Shakespeare all make use of the ensemble troupe in everything from *Much Ado About Nothing* to *King Lear*. An ensemble cast is a group of actors who play a set of equally important characters. Ensemble casts are a common convention of teen movies, as they allow the introduction of a groups of young actors, some of whom may go on to become 'A-List' actors. Films such as *American Graffiti* (1973, dir. George Lucas) or *Top Gun* (1986, dir. Tony Scott), helped launch the careers of Harrison Ford and Tom Cruise, for instance. The ensemble cast, more often than not, is used in teen 'slasher' films (for example, *The Faculty*, 1998, dir. Robert Rodriguez), where it is useful to have a large cast capable of putting their heart (sometimes literally) into a small role as they

meet a variety of inventive deaths. Such films often introduce future stars to the waiting audience – or not.

A big star in an ensemble cast can sometimes overshadow the film. One way to solve that is to have *lots* of big stars (*Ocean's Eleven*, 2001, dir. Steven Soderbergh, *The Magnificent Seven*, 1960, dir. John Sturges) or not to have any at all and risk the enterprise not succeeding.

The Usual Suspects uses an ensemble cast, although these are older men and the intention was not so much to introduce them to cinema audiences but to create the impression of a real ensemble, a group of experienced and different men who each bring real character to their roles. That did leave the producer and director of the film with a problem though. In *Nothing is What It Seems: The Making of The Usual Suspects* (TV documentary, 1998) Bryan Singer describes standing in the queue at the Sundance Festival and being approached by a woman who asked him if he knew anything about the film *The Usual Suspects*, most particularly she wanted to know who was in it. He began to list the cast, she considered it and decided against the screening – she wanted the security of a known actor to persuade her to see a movie. In that case she made a mistake.

Genre likes its big stars. It follows that if an audience feels secure buying a ticket for a type of story they understand, they are likely to be more secure watching somebody in it whose performances they like.

However, *The Usual Suspects* is unusual as an ensemble movie since it employed actors who were not entirely unknown, and all of whom were experienced professionals. It was the writer, director and editor/composer who had limited experience. The ensemble when it works allows each actor an individual role which contributes to the whole piece. It does also perhaps allow the adventure of personality that we see in Benicio del Toro's performance as the outrageously accented and camp Fenster. All the actors credit the film as a

NOTES:

fine example of an ensemble cast. Gabriel Bryne likens the experience to being a band that had a great hit in days gone by; a camaraderie between the characters is clear in the performances and it works for the actors as colleagues throughout their professional lives. All of the actors stated that it was rare for a film to achieve that sense of an ensemble. So rare, in fact, that it was only the second year that the National Board of Review awards in the USA had a category of Best Ensemble. It was awarded in that year to in the main cast of *The Usual Suspects*.[8]

The Heist

The heist movie lends itself inevitably to the use of an ensemble cast. Heists take a team to organise them. The conventions of a heist movie include a robbery of some kind that has the advantage of vast rewards obtained in the face of some danger. The execution of the heist requires elaborate plans, professional skills applied to the task, and tension in the moments when things do not quite go according to plan. Unlike many straightforward psychological or detective thrillers, heist movies quite often let one or all of the perpetrators get away with their spoils (*The Italian Job*, 2003, dir. F. Gary Gray); at the very least the audience is left wondering as to the success of the task, as they are at the end of *The Italian Job* (1969, dir. Peter Collinson). The traditional conventions of the thriller have dictated that at the end of the film there must be resolution, most particularly the kind of resolution that re-establishes the ideology to which we ascribe as a society – that crime does not pay. This is hegemony, often known in the trade as the controlling idea. It is the accepted philosophy which our society and culture agree by consensus to implement: romantic love, work ethic, tolerance, crime and punishment, freedom. Unfortunately, heist movies quite often challenge the hegemony of crime and punishment: in terms of most heists in the movies crime *does* pay – crime can be quite lucrative; in addition, we want our criminals to get away with it.

The Twist

Clever plots and groups of people allow more opportunity for that most lauded of thriller conventions, the twist. A group of people who may have reason not to trust each other and a plan that involves murder and a lot of money allow the clever writer the opportunity to deceive the audience, and *The Usual Suspects* makes famous use of this thriller convention.

Additional Noir Characters

The sleuth is a common convention of thriller and noir. In a noir the sleuth is often a little flawed, inclined to smoke and drink and is definitely cynical. There is no finer portrayal of the noir sleuth than that of Sam Spade as portrayed by Humphrey Bogart in *The Maltese Falcon* or Bogart as Philip Marlowe in *The Big Sleep* (1946, dir. Howard Hawks). The character appears only as cameo in *The Usual Suspects*, but down to the cigarette, the cynicism and the hat the FBI Agent Jack Baer played by Giancarlo Esposito is a classic noir sleuth, only his colour is a slight reinvention of the noir convention. Agent Dave Kujan, played by Chazz Palminteri, offers a version of the sleuth, but his lack of noir cynicism does not qualify him for the role of noir detective.

Narration

From the gravel voiced narrations of Humphrey Bogart to the slurred storytelling of Deckard in the noir sci-fi *Blade Runner*, a convention of noir has been the narrator: the character who tells the story either as an observer or as a key character. The use of non-diegetic narration (sound that does not come from the location – see Chapter 4) and the snappy, cynical dialogue played out between characters that are, in themselves flawed, are cited by the Executive Producer, Robert Jones, as reflective of the style of noir and it is part of what attracted him to the script.

The analysis of the shots in Table 2.1 demonstrates some of the typical noir elements in *The Usual Suspects*; in Table 2.2 the analysis demonstrates aspects of the narrative represented by the images that hint at the mythical nature of the story and its characters.

NOTES:

8.   http://www.nbrmp.org/awards/

Table 2.1 The Semiotics of Noir: *The Usual Suspects*

Image	Noir	
The silhouette as the character climbs down the ladder. DVD Chapter 2: Time Code 00:04:35.	The silhouette has all the semiotics of a noir character. The trench coat, the trilby; the fact that we never see his face. He is the faceless evil that we all fear, light is the enemy of noir. It reveals all – even the bad guy. One of the most famous revelations in noir film is the appearance of Harry Lime in **The Third Man** (1949, dir. Carol Reed). This representation of Keyser Soze is melodramatic and stylised but it is film noir.	
The cigarette. DVD Chapter 2: Time Code 00:04:26.	The cigarette is a strong signifier of noir. In noir women it indicated their moral ambivalence. It indicated the heat of passion. In **The Usual Suspects** it reveals the killer's identity to Dean Keaton (Gabriel Byrne), but it also drops a clue in the narrative for Dave Kujan. The lighter is used to set fire to the police car later in the narrative, which was said to be Dean Keaton's idea by Verbal Kint; and Dave Kujan used it for his narrative (see Chapter 4).	
Dean Keaton's arrest. High-angle shot on the table. DVD Chapter 3: Time Code 00:07:11.	The rat-in-the-trap shot is not exclusive to film noir, but it has been widely used, not least by Hitchcock in **North by Northwest** (1959) who portrayed Roger Thornhill running from the UN building by using a matte painted shot that made it look as though he was being filmed from the top of the building. In this scene the idea is to make the character look trapped. The angle is extreme, the character of Dean Keaton is dressed in a light suit, to suggest his innocence, but he is trapped. Like many noir characters he is doomed from this moment on to find that things just get worse and worse and is partly his own fault.	
Deep focus. Venetian blinds. Bridges. The visual lie. DVD Chapter 19: Time Code 00:48.44	Gabriel Byrne said in **Nothing is What it Seems** that Singer used every technique he knew to make the film work. This shot is a classic example of a noir shot. It is deep focus – everything is in focus and both the characters face towards the camera not each other. Another excellent shot is 00:35:58 Kajun and Rabin Venetian blinds have a referent – bars: they look like prison. They cast shadows like bars, they hint at prison. Bridges – light is often used as a bridge to compound the connection between the characters. Here the light on the blinds, the blinds themselves and the books on the sofa bridge the two characters. The visual lie – here Verbal Kint, looks small, distant and vulnerable. He is filmed like this throughout the scenes in the office. A small ordinary man, often looking up or cowering, never looking powerful. Only on one or two of the extreme close ups is there a hint of something else.	
The doppelgänger shot. DVD Chapter 24: Time Code 01:10:05.	The dopplegänger shot is the reflection shot. A dopplegänger is an evil double, said to be attached to every individual; it is your other evil self. When a doppelgänger shot is used it is to hint at a hidden self. It is not exclusive to noir and Hitchcock uses it in **Psycho** when Janet Leigh enters the bathroom at the car lot, to count her money; she is both shot as a rat-in-the-trap and in front of a mirror.	

NOTES:

The Usual Suspects as Neo Noir

Table 2.2 The Semiotics of *The Usual Suspects* as Neo Noir

Image	Neo noir
The referent. DVD Chapter 24: Time Code 01:09:14.	This shot poses Mr Koyobashi in mid close up to the left of the screen with an up-lighter on the wall. The set no doubt was not dressed, but shot in true noir style on locations, but the light has a referent. It looks like a medieval torch, a flame. It hints at an ancient world and an ancient evil.
The light. DVD Chapter 26: Time Code 01:18:27.	As Todd Hockney turns to take his last breath he is bathed in what may be a supernatural light.
The fires of hell. DVD Chapter 22: Time Code 00:59:03.	Keyser Soze is silhouetted against the fires of hell, his long hair flowing, portrayed as such after a particularly vicious act – super villain, an antagonist or a myth?
The Korean Friendship Bell. DVD Chapter 18: Time Code 00:46:58.	This is a strangely exotic location for the suspects to meet but as the scene commences it is one of the very few moments in the film when Verbal Kint is filmed from a low angle. He is framed by the pagoda roof; it makes him look powerful, mysterious, slightly devilish.

NOTES:

WHO'S WHO?

It's quite common and quite understandable for students to get mixed up with 'who's who' amongst the suspects so the following is a quick quiz:

TEACHER'S COPY

Question	Answer
Who is the first suspect to wear a red shirt?	Fred Fenster.
Which two suspects have a beard?	Todd Hockney and McManus.
What does Todd Hockney do (his job)?	Car mechanic.
Who limps?	Verbal Kint.
Who was meant to be dead?	Dean Keaton.
Who's office do they use for the interview?	Sergeant Rabin.
What law enforcement agency does Dave Kujan work for?	Customs and Excise.
Which two suspects have had a longstanding relationship?	McManus and Fenster.
Who smokes a cigar?	FBI Agent Jack Baer.
What is the name of Keyser Soze's lawyer?	Mr Koyabashi.
Who's the girl?	Edie Finneran.
What did Todd Hockney do that sparked the whole line up off?	Stole a truck full of explosives (see snooker room scene).
Who is their fence in LA?	Redfoot.
Who is first to die?	Fenster.
Who is the marksman?	McManus.
Who is good with explosives?	Hockney.
Who has a girlfriend?	Dean Keaton.
Who wears the red shirt in the snooker room?	Dean Keaton.

WHO'S WHO?

STUDENT COPY

Question	Answer
Who is the first suspect to wear a red shirt?	
Which two suspects have a beard?	
What does Todd Hockney do (his job)?	
Who limps?	
Who was meant to be dead?	
Who's office do they use for the interview?	
What law enforcement agency does Dave Kujan work for?	
Which two suspects have had a longstanding relationship?	
Who smokes a cigar?	
What is the name of Keyser Soze's lawyer?	
Who's the girl?	
What did Todd Hockney do that sparked the whole line up off?	
Who is their fence in LA?	
Who is first to die?	
Who is the marksman?	
Who is good with explosives?	
Who has a girlfriend?	
Who wears the red shirt in the snooker room?	

ENSEMBLE

Internet Research

On the internet, go into the National Board of Review (www.nbrmp.org) and look at the number of films that have been given the award for Best Acting by an Ensemble:

- Is there a common genre?

- What other genre's are represented?

- What are the differences between ensemble films?

- What elements are the same?

- What for you are the essential elements of an ensemble film?

What could be the benefits of an ensemble cast for the following:

- Audiences?

- The cast?

Who would be your ideal ensemble cast and why?

TASK

It is very common for screenplay and TV writers to write 'back stories' for the characters they represent in a story. The audience may never be aware of the back story, but the existence of that story means that the writer has a clear understanding of the character they are portraying and how they might react in certain situations. Dean Keaton's back story is hinted at but what about more detail or the back story of one of the others? Start with the explanations of each suspect given by Verbal Kint, choose one of the suspects and write a back story for them. Include the following:

- Where they were born?

- What their childhood was like?

- Education they received?

- A talent or a hobby they have?

- What relationships they had or have?

- What their major flaws are?

- What led them into crime?

CHAPTER 2 GLOSSARY: TEACHER

Term	Definition
Auteur theory	The idea that a director 'authors' a film, that his/her personality and philosophy are evident in the product.
Controlling ideology	Similar to hegemony but used in media to identify the way media remains within certain philosophical ideals – crime does not or should not pay.
Conventions	The characteristics that repeat themselves in a film, such as common plotlines, mise-en-scène, common characters that define the category of film.
Ensemble	A group of performers who share an equal role in the creation of a dramatic piece.
Femme fatale	A central female figure in thrillers who is dangerous to know – she is likely to use sex to tempt men to further corruption.
Film noir	'Dark film' applied particularly to a style of film shot predominantly in the 40s and 50s, using low lighting, location filming and 'dark' storylines.
Genre	A category of media, in this case film, that is defined by certain common characteristics.
Hegemony	The predominant idea or influence particularly from the state of cultural consensus.
Heist	A robbery usually conducted by a group of people.
Twist	The unexpected shift in the plot that surprises an audience.

GENRE CHART

Choose a film within these genres, fill in the title and identify the genre element by filling in the boxes.

	Romantic Comedy Title:	Science Fiction Title:
Conventions		
Codes		
Representations of main characters		
A-list actors		
Mise-en-scène		
Narrative structure • Narrative theory/ binary/codes Disruption and quest • Plot similarities		
Audience expectations		

UK TOP 10 2005

Look at the table below and complete the following:

- Define the genre each film is in.

- Define some of the codes and conventions that are used by the relevant genre.

- See if there is any correlation between the production company and the genre.

- See if there are any stars appearing in more than one film in the list.

- Think of a film that is not in the top ten and try to establish why it's not there.

- Ask yourself, do you like any of those films? Are you a genre addict or an independent cinema-goer?

- See if you can name one film this year that does not fit a genre.

Film	Distributor	Box Office (millions)
Harry Potter & the Goblet of Fire	Warner Brothers	£45.8
Star Wars Episode III: Revenge of the Sith	20th Century Fox	£39.3
Charlie and the Chocolate Factory	Warner Brothers	£37.4
The Chronicles of Narnia	BVI	£32.0
Wallace & Gromit: The Curse of the Were-Rabbit	UIP	£31.9
War of the Worlds	UIP	£30.5
Meet the Fockers	UIP	£28.7
Madagascar	UIP	£22.7
King Kong	UIP	£20.3
Hitch	Sony Pictures	£17.4

Source: Pearl & Dean.

FILM NOIR

TASK

Identify two or three classic film noirs from the list below. If you can, watch them; if not, read about them and attempt to do a flow chart of the plot. See what conventions repeat themselves. Would you say these are the conventions of a film noir? If so, why?

Possible titles:

- *Double Indemnity*.

- *Body Heat*.

- *The Postman Always Rings Twice*.

- *The Big Combo*.

- *The Maltese Falcon*.

- *The Big Sleep*.

- *Detour*.

Discuss why you think *The Usual Suspects* is a neo noir and why, in some respects, it is not.

Any English or media student of quite a young age should now be aware that stories have a structure. The earliest fairy tales begin with 'Once upon a time' and once the story has begun there is an expectation, in most students, that it will have a beginning, a middle and an end; but that, as they say, is not the end of it at all. The role of narrative in film and TV has become a huge part of the study of what used to be called storytelling. Constraints of time, commercial breaks, cast requirements and audience satisfaction all influence any film-maker. This has been combined with the increased study of the role of narrative in literature and philosophy. This means that narrative itself could be a narrative of its own, like a play within a play, and one of the exceptional aspects of *The Usual Suspects* is that it offers an exceptional narrative; in fact, it offers at least two exceptional narratives.

For the media student to understand how the narrative conventions work or are challenged in *The Usual Suspects* it is useful to have a few narrative theories to hand that apply to many genres but most particularly to the thriller genre.

Linear Narrative

Before applying academic names to narrative theories it is worth making sure that students have an understanding of **linear** and **non-linear** narrative. The fairy tale structure suggested above lends itself to the definition of linear narrative: a beginning, a middle and an end. The narrative literally travels in a line, offering the storytelling in chronological order. Even a story where two stories, or aspects of a story, are told separately while leading to the same conclusion can be considered linear. Some films such as *The Straight Story* (1999) directed by David Lynch uses the idea of linear narrative, in the same way as Lynch deals with non-linear narratives in his earlier film *Lost Highway* (1997).

Non-Linear Narrative

The concept of non-linear narrative might be easy to grasp but it is certainly more difficult to read and to analyse. The most obvious use of the non-linear narrative might be the use of the flashback, although that is usually a device for containing two linear narratives in one story. Perhaps the most obvious mark of the non-linear narrative is that it may not resolve itself in one conclusion; that it will tell its story from many different points of view, which at the finish of the film may not have resolution such that the narrative can be truly regarded as non-linear. In this regard the work of Woody Allen might be seen as an attempt to narrate non-linear stories.

The Case for Non-Linear

The Usual Suspects starts at the end and this is not atypical of films in a variety of genres. In novels, films, poetry and plays the narrative will start with a portrayal of the end scene or with a storyteller who is about to tell the audience of what they have just seen or experienced. This does not on its own make the narrative non-linear.

What makes *The Usual Suspects* overall narrative non-linear is the fact that it contains several narratives. An analysis of narratives identifies the following:

- The story told by Verbal Kint in the office.

- The tracking of the narrative from the boat to the fax through Agent Jack Baer.

- The story of Dean Keaton told by Dave Kujan.

- The story of the story being told.

- *The Usual Suspects* as Linear Narrative

By the very nature of its twist *The Usual Suspects* does lead up to something: it sets us a mystery, misdirects our eye and, with consummate skill, it offers us an unexpected ending. In that sense it has a beginning, a middle and an end. It also has a chronology that can be sorted; it works as follows without the need for narrative input from the interview in the office:

NOTES:

Time and Narrative

- A robbery we never see takes place.

- The suspects are picked up for the line up.

- They decide to kick back at the authorities and stage a heist.

- They do so well they get another commission.

- This one goes wrong and they are approached by the agent of Keyser Soze, who claims to have been after them all along.

- They are blackmailed into staging another heist, against fellow criminals – a heist which has a very low chance of success.

- One of their number breaks ranks and is killed.

- They try and fail to avenge his killing.

- They are still locked into the heist on the boat.

- The heist takes place and all but Verbal Kint and the Hungarian are killed.

- Verbal Kint is arrested and interrogated.

- The Hungarian names Keyser Soze.

- Verbal Kint clears his name.

- Dave Kujan realises he has been fooled – too late.

But if the story were to be told as a linear narrative without the cutaways to the interrogation, that takes place on a different timeline, would it be the same film?

Whether or not the narrative of *The Usual Suspects* fits with either linear or non-linear definitions, it is important to remember that the whole point of the film is that it is precisely that – a narrative. The tale told to Dave Kujan is a story, cobbled together from bits of information in the office. The writer Christopher McQuarrie also owns up to using precisely that technique, when in three days he had to knock together a decent pitch.

Characters as Narrative

In the narrative theories to follow, a description of certain kinds of characters as they relate to stories will become obvious, but at this stage it is probably best to guide students towards the use of appropriate language when referring to main characters. The words 'heroes' and 'villains' are rather too archetypal for the realistic narratives that most thrillers portray. The characters that lead such plots are rarely flawless either as pure good or as pure evil. Better definitions of such characters are:

- Protagonist – the character that is given the problem to solve. This is the character that the audience identifies with. It is their journey, their quest that the audience follows and they pursue the protagonist as a central character. More often than not a true protagonist must reveal themselves early on to be a little flawed, perhaps a liar, or a sceptic, but these flaws will be the very aspects of their character that will enable them to survive and win, precisely because they are flawed.

- Antagonist – this character is the enemy. This is the character who poses the problem. The antagonist is the one who disrupts the equilibrium and sets the tone of the story. Traditionally he/she is the bad guy, who, in the end, should be defeated.

Narrative Theories

It is not essential for a media student up to AS or A2 Level to apply named theories to the work they study. Linear and non-linear may be enough, but it is difficult to introduce them to the subject of narrative theory without referring to the work of others, so it is appropriate (if only as an extension task) to offer the names and theories and how they apply.

English students at a higher level may have come across Bruno Bettelheim's 'The Uses of Enchantment: The Meaning and Importance of Fairytales'[9] – a discussion of the nature and narrative of fairy tales and magic. The fairy tale is a good place to start, although only the most motivated of students will find comfort in Bettelheim whose work is not directed specifically at the media. However, most media narrative theories have been taken from those theories that have discussed the nature of storytelling or the myth making in our society, and not the properties of TV and film-making which have their own specific constraints.

NOTES:

9. Bruno Bettelheim, *The Uses of Enchantment: The Meaning and Importance of Fairytales* (London: Penguin, 1991).

The theorists I recommend here are those recommended largely by 'The Media Student's Book'.[10] However there are one or two additional aspects of narrative theory that can be applied specifically to *The Usual Suspects*, but first the line up of the usual narrative suspects.

The Usual Narratives

Vladimir Propp (1895–1970) published 'Morphology of the Folktale' in 1928. His aim was to break down the constituent elements of the narratives of common and repeated tales to see how they differed and, more importantly, how they were similar to one another. The similarities extended beyond the obvious announcement of 'Once upon a time…'. The similarities applied to characters, to their size, shape and gender, even to their names and their tasks. (Who hasn't got Sleeping Beauty and Snow White mixed up on occasions?) What Propp had spotted was evidence of genre and he proceeded to examine how that genre worked in the stories we all read in terms of the codes and conventions that he identified they contained. In all, he came up with a variety of actions and functions that he considered were common elements that fulfilled the genre of the fairy tale.

Remember that this analysis applies to fairy tales and myths; the characters take on an archetypal capacity, they are heroes and villains as opposed to protagonists and antagonists.

Typically fairy tales involve a king who sets the task, the task itself, the prince or hero, the princess, who is also the prize, and many variations on that theme.

A more detailed breakdown of the characters is as follows:

1) The villain.

2) The hero.

3) The donor (who provides an object with magic properties).

4) The helper (partner).

5) The princess (obviously).

6) The father (rewards the hero).

7) The dispatcher (sends the hero on his way).

8) The false hero (the jilted lover, maybe).

The essential thing to remember when studying narrative this closely when it is related to fairy tales is to remember that, in a sense, *all* stories are fairy tales. There is no doubt that the film world offers fantasy and science fiction stories such as *Star Wars Episode IV* (1977) that offer demonstrable applications of Propp's theories, but once the student is familiar with the theory they should be able to see that it applies to a variety of film narratives, even those that represent social realism or at the very least offer some form of verisimilitude.

One example of a modern film narrative that works very well with Propp's theory is *Speed* (1994, dir. Jan de Bont). This narrative is set against the backdrop of a contemporary Los Angeles, but it has a prince, a villain, a false hero, a donor and it certainly has a princess who, in true fairy tale style, ends up tied to a post while

Action/function	Narrative element
Preparation	Which could be roughly transposed as 'it all starts to go wrong.'
Complication	Somebody gets hurt.
Transference	The hero has to start to sort it out.
Struggle	Things start to get sorted out.
Return	The hero returns.
Recognition	The hero says 'I told you so.'

NOTES:

10. Gill Branston and Roy Stafford (eds), *The Media Student's Book* (London: Routledge, 2002).

the prince beheads the dragon – check it out, I promise you it is all there.

Propp's theories were considered so dangerous at the time of publication in his native Russia that it was suppressed by the Soviet government; as one of nature's great propagandists, Stalin knew the danger of analysing information too closely. It would not take a good media student long to discover the flaws in a propagandist narrative.

The Usual Suspects and Propp: Is The Usual Suspects a fairy tale?

At first sight it seems not: there is no princess, there is no prince driven on a quest to rescue, there is no one willing to set a task, and nobody seems to be in the least bit helpful. Not only that, but the film's ethos of verisimilitude in terms of the currency of New York gangsters and their relationships to the police and customs essentially means that there is no sign of the positive hue that a fantastical tale might portray – but look again.

The villain/antagonist – even people who have not seen the film know the name of Keyser Soze, the unseen, possibly unidentified villain of the piece. He is so evil that he could murder his own wife and children to save not only his life, but his reputation. There is some suggestion that Keyser Soze is not just a villain but a super-villain. In this he has something in common with the villains of comic books and so, it is perhaps, no surprise to note that Bryan Singer went on to direct the *X-Men* (2003).

Perhaps the strongest evidence that *The Usual Suspects* is, in fact, a fairy tale, may well rest in the stylised violence committed by the long-haired silhouette of Keyser Soze. Just as the trilby and the trench coated silhouette of the shooter on the boat references the history of noir films, so the figure of Keyser Soze, long-haired and framed by fire conjures up visions of hell, of dark princes, desperate dragons and a medieval philosophy of life. The semiotics of the scene where Verbal describes the legend of Keyser Soze, distances the violence and tells the story in a different style. Keyser Soze's exaggerated evil, provides the story with a fairy tale element, a hint of supernatural darkness and it enables Verbal to play a sleight of hand and look afraid and small, completely unlike the villain he describes. Moreover, in retrospect, it is so extreme that it allows us to wonder whether any of it is true, whether it is all a fairy tale.

- The hero/protagonist – we have a law enforcement officer, Dave Kujan (Customs), who, in the tradition of all true heroes, has a quest, a quest to find the truth and thus defeat the dragon.

- The donor – Mr Kobayashi provides them with the information and the motivation to complete the task and his object with magical properties is the briefcase of blackmail that defines each suspect's life and binds him to the mission set by Keyser Soze.

- The helper – may be Sergeant Jeff Rabin. He provides the office and is at Dave Kujan's side most of the time.

- The dispatcher – that is more difficult, but it does not always have to be a character; in fact, the police department of the FBI is a possible contender. They set up the scenario whereby the hero is dispatched on his task of solving crime.

- The princess – Edie Finneran, blonde and beautiful and definitely a damsel in distress, although it is true to say that hers is not a fairy tale ending.

- The false hero – is even more difficult, partly because *The Usual Suspects* is full of false hero's, but agent Jack Baer may be the correct contender. He is on the scene of the crime and initially identifies the presence of Keyser Soze but does that information help or hinder the quest?

NOTES:

Does Keyser Soze even exist?

It is perhaps the exaggerated nature of the villainhood of Keyser Soze that turns him into a giant and makes the story of **The Usual Suspects** more like a fairy tale. A villain who might be evil itself, the devil with a human face, that is the stuff of folk tales. This might make him an archetype, a character so universal, so much larger than life that he is no longer real but representative of the concept of arbitrary evil or, in this case, the case for revenge. The term archetype was used by Carl Gustav Jung to describe such characters and it has been applied by Propp to both narrative and character.

In fact Keyser Soze may not be such an exaggerated character after all. Bryan Singer and Christopher McQuarrie were brought up only a few miles from one of America's most notorious murderers. In 1971 John List murdered his wife, mother and three teenage children, then disappeared for 18 years. The highly popular series *America's Most Wanted* in 1989 used technology to remodel his older face and he was found out, remarried and living under the name of Robert Clark. He was an ordinary man, an accountant and church-goer. He committed a heinous crime during the childhoods of these two men and then disappeared to who knew where? As they grew up all that was left was List's ability to haunt their dreams and imagination.

Once you understand that story then it seems that Keyser Soze is not only a possible human villain, but one who is represented with verisimilitude. Nevertheless, the combination of actual evil and mystery is potent mix for the creation of a myth.

Tzvetan Todorov

Born in 1939 Todorov's discussion of narrative has been an exposition of literature rather than a specific analysis of filmic narratives ('The Poetics of Prose'[11]). In addition his approach is structuralist in terms of the narrative theory that is most commonly referred to amongst media students. In recent years he has developed a more postmodern approach to the construction of

historical narrative and continues to lecture on that theme. However, for the purposes of media theory, his analysis of narrative offers a simple but effective breakdown of the construction of most media narratives. The analysis is as follows:

1) The narrative starts in a state of equilibrium.

2) That equilibrium is disrupted in some way.

3) There is a recognition that there has been some disruption.

4) There is an attempt to repair that disruption.

5) There is a resolution and reinstatement of that equilibrium.

The new equilibrium is often qualified by some kind of moral change, redemption or a knowledge that the characters adhere to that they did not before. Shakespeare knew this; at the end of *Hamlet*, Fortinbras wanders into the mayhem and (in paraphrase) announces 'XXX! What happened here? Let's make sure it doesn't happen again'. In *Romeo and Juliet* the families swear to be reconciled as a consequence of the death of the two lovers; their lives cannot be restored but the equilibrium disrupted by feuding can be restored.

Todorov's narrative theory is easy for any student to recognise. It is most commonly used in episodic television series, such **Buffy, Smallville** and now our own **Dr Who** – to mention but a few. Quite often the first two elements of the narrative are contained in the moments before the titles are run.

Todorov and *The Usual Suspects*

In **The Usual Suspects** Todorov does apply but, as we have seen, the narrative is not linear and it is not merely non-linear either. The narrative begins in the middle of disruption: the equilibrium in the film is that brief moment in the film just before the suspects are picked up for the line-up and, from there on in, the narrative shifts into deeper and deeper disruption. The resolution at the end, whilst possibly one of the most satisfying surprises in film history, does not resolve anything; in fact, it may not even solve

NOTES:

11. T. Todorov, *The Poetics of Prose* (trans. from the French by Richard Howard; with a new foreword by Jonathan Culler), (Oxford: Blackwell, 1977).

Time and Narrative

anything, the enigma remains which points to the next theorist.

Roland Barthes (1915–80)

Barthes was a post-structuralist theorist (although not a postmodernist) and he challenged accepted ideas in media theory with regard to ideas of realism that included naturalism and innocence. He concluded that the media's idea of reality was myth; not just 'a myth', but myth itself.

Barthes is responsible for introducing the concepts of denotation and connotation (see Chapter 1):

Denotation is the first order of signification – that which is actually there.

Connotation is the second order of meaning – the implications or connotations of what is there – often bound by cultural influences and ideas (hegemony). These are the evaluative meanings, the creation of myth.

This idea of myth reflects the ideas put in place by Claude Lévi-Strauss who discussed time and narrative. He defined a narrative as either bound by time, one that is told and read word by word and cannot be changed, and one that, through a single concept can have meaning throughout time. Barthes' first two codes listed below apply to narratives bound by time; the final three have a closer relationship to those narratives whose meaning is not bound by time.

Barthes, however, did not simplify his theory as much as Strauss did. He applied to the analysis of narrative the idea of **five codes**:

The hermeneutic code: The creation of the puzzle or the enigma. Without an enigma, says Barthes, a narrative struggles to retain its audience's interest. In common with Todorov's observation that equilibrium is disrupted and Propp's observation that tasks and challenges are set, Barthes suggests that all this creates an enigma. Part of any narrative is the attempt to reconstruct the story presented by the enigma.

The proairetic code: The presence of action with a narrative, especially action which leads to further action or raises further enigmas. When the protagonist raises his/her fist it begs the question 'What will happen next?'

The semic code: This code is related much more to language (semantics) and to connotations. It is the code that applies to characters and how they are described both in language and in semiotics (the language of images).

The symbolic code: This is not as simple as suggesting that the image of a dove symbolises peace, although the same principle is at work. At its simplest it refers to what might be regarded as subtext. The story is told in language that has surface meaning, but that story may symbolise other realities such as the battle between good and evil, or the struggle between the powerless and the powerful – think for example of the many layers of meaning to the simple story of David and Goliath.

The referential code: A reference to the cultural influences on a narrative. The presence of a controlling ideology that shapes the narrative such that good defeats evil, work is seen to be better than unemployment or that blood is thicker than water.

Barthes and The *Usual Suspects*

The Usual Suspects is probably one of the most enigmatic films around, to the extent that some might argue it is incomprehensible.

The first scene of the film manages to cover all five codes in one brief moment:

Hermeneutic – who is the shooter and why is he shooting the man (Dean Keaton) who seems to know who he is and why he will shoot?

Proairetic – the gunman kills the wounded man without mercy and then runs away. Such an action begs the question, what will happen next?

NOTES:

Semic – the shooter is in silhouette, with a trench coat and a trilby hat on. The scene is dark; the language of murder is there.

Symbolic – the direct use of silhouette as he runs away connotes or symbolises the faceless evil of all human beings. The victim smokes a last cigarette before his firing squad and as the perpetrator leaves he sets the fires of hell, both punishing and purifying.

Referential – once again, the hat and coat need no explanation; neither does the cigarette or the darkness: all our cultural understanding tells the viewer that this is a dark story, set in a noir style (even if we don't fully understand the concept of noir).

Claude Lévi-Strauss

Claude Lévi-Strauss's[12] theory offers a complementary study to the ideas put forth by Saussure. Saussure studied language, Lévi-Strauss studied anthropology and behaviour:

'This idea is at the heart of any kind of structuralist analysis. Saussure applies it to language; Lévi-Strauss applies it as an anthropologist, to kinship systems, cultural organizations, and to myth; Roland Barthes… applies this system to a wide variety of contemporary Western (mostly French) cultural "signs," including food, advertising, and clothing'. Mary Klages[13]

Both Saussure and Lévi-Strauss were convinced that by applying a structuralist philosophy or system to the object of their study they could discover certain basic human truths and Lévi-Strauss felt these truths were very simple and self-evident. Lévi-Strauss contended that the art of myth making could be distilled into tiny units or building blocks of myths which he called **mythemes**. This was to reflect the title given to the smallest unit of stable meaning in language – morphemes (phonemes in speech). Mythemes, however, differ slightly in the relation to myths. Lévi-Strauss argues that you can read stories in the two following ways:

With time: The reader makes a chronological attempt to read the text, word by word, in real time; time that they cannot reverse.

At once: The reader absorbs the meaning in one look. This form of reading can be timeless; it can be the same yesterday, today and forever.

'If you don't read the sentence, but rather think of it as being the structure of English, it exists in a single moment, every moment – yesterday as well as today as well as tomorrow. That's reversible time.'[14]

Myths then are made of units that are put together with respect to certain rules and those rules function on a simplistic relationship with each other that makes use of binary opposites.

Lévi-Strauss argues that whatever story we think of there will be a binary opposite to the initial structure; in essence, our stories are about solving problems. If a class is told to write a story about making a cake their objective will be identical and that is that they go from 'no cake' to 'cake'. Each student will write a different story as to how they came to make the cake, but each student will deal with the same binary opposite, bringing a certain kind of order out of chaos. In fact the effort by humankind to do precisely that is the essence of their binary; myth making is an attempt to make sense out of contradictions and the ultimate contradiction, according to Lévi-Strauss, is the one between life and death, the ultimate binary. The other one, which is much more evident in *The Usual Suspects*, is that between good and evil.

NOTES:

12. Dr. Mary Klages, Associate Professor of English, University of Colorado at Boulder, 'Claude Lévi-Strauss: The Structural Study of Myth and Other Structuralist Ideas', http://www.colorado.edu/English/engl2010mk/levistrauss.2001.htm.

13. Ibid.

14. Ibid.

Time and Narrative

Oppositions in *The Usual Suspects*

In fact, the application of Lévi-Strauss's binary to *The Usual Suspects* is not quite as clear cut as it might be were the student to apply it to *Star Wars*, or *Alien*, or *Speed*. The first impression of the suspects is that they are all bad and that the police are not much better. The idea that there is an overwhelming battle between good and evil going on seems lost in the malaise of gangster agendas, verisimilitude and a host of selfish motivations that may or may not be true. However, if we look closer:

The Usual Suspects Binary Table

The Police/Customs	The Suspects
The woman (Edie Finneran)	The man (Dean Keaton)
The truth (sought by Dave Kujan)	The falsehood (told by Verbal Kint)
Verbal Kint	Keyser Soze
Dean Keaton (going straight)	Dean Keaton (the corrupt policeman)
Good (Dave Kujan)	Evil (Keyser Soze)

the essence of binary is not that it can be located in straightforward black and white concepts but that it relates to the idea of narrative as timeless. The inner contest within a human being to do the right thing is a timeless narrative, the method of telling it through the character of Dean Keaton is the narrative that is locked in time. The idea of an evil so fearful that it destroys even that which it loves, has always been set against the effectiveness attributed to the efforts of honourable men to destroy such evil, without becoming corrupted by it. The contradiction of method, the idea that the pursuer does not become as bestial as the pursued, is also timeless, but that very aspiration reduces the power of the good to overcome the evil.

Seeing What You Want To See: Phenomenology

Whilst the theories listed above might be complex for some students to analyse and apply not just to *The Usual Suspects*, but to any narrative, filmic or otherwise, one approach that might more easily be applied to the film is the concept of phenomenology. While definitions of phenomenology may vary from existentialist ideas to neural studies, the idea is simple. We see what we want to see in a narrative and this is often governed by our own self-interest or the influences upon us.

Kujan and the crucial coffee cup

The chronological narrative of *The Usual Suspects* may not be linear but there is one very clear linear narrative in the film and that is the story told by Agent Dave Kujan. He tells this story in the traditional convention of the detective film genre. Kujan has gathered all the information together and he decides at last that he knows the identity of the great antagonist, Keyser Soze. He tells this story to Verbal Kint. The narrative is edited together in a mini linear narrative form, using images and even lip sync as Kujan announces that the trench-coated silhouette who shot Dean Keaton is none other than Dean Keaton himself.

NOTES:

Bryan Singer and John Ottman recount the story of trying to persuade Gabriel Byrne to shoot the scene when he clearly read it as nonsense, since he was the one being shot. The narrative *is* nonsense, of course, but not to Dave Kujan who once believed Dean Keaton to be dead when he was not, and now cannot believe he is dead when the one thing that Verbal Kint is likely to be telling the truth about is precisely that.

A classic exercise in the function of phenomenology of the film is to look at the scene where Verbal is left in the office on his own for the first time (DVD Chapter 9 (first scene), Time Code 00:21:03).

He does nothing; he just sits and looks. When the viewer first sees this scene, they see a man who is bored, perhaps afraid, waiting to be interviewed by the police. When they see the film for a second time they see a man concocting a story. A man looking round the office and taking in every detail, so that once Verbal becomes verbal, he can convince his interrogator that he is merely a pawn in a big criminal's plan.

John Ottman and Bryan Singer believed it was absolutely necessary to include this second narrative and they set up an extra shoot to add that to that narrative to complete Verbal Kint's sleight of hand. It was a classic exposition of the action of phenomenology on an individual's personal narrative.

In the end Dave Kujan was so determined to pin the crimes on Dean Keaton he allowed himself to read the story he was told as an indictment of Dean Keaton, and only just a moment too late does he realise his mistake. He wanted so much to believe that Dean Keaton was his antagonist that

he never even took a moment to look around the room. His controlling ideas, his hegemony, were imposed on the story Verbal told. All Verbal had to do was agree with him. The sad truth is that some people never realise their mistake – even Gabriel Byrne said at Cannes that he was not absolutely convinced that his character was *not* Keyser Soze. Needless to say the cast and crew like to encourage the mystery that surrounds the character of Keyser Soze, it is good for the film sales.

After all 'The greatest trick the Devil ever pulled was convincing the world that he did not exist' (Verbal Kint, suggesting that the Devil understands phenomenology).

NOTES:

Classroom Worksheets

They Might be Giants – or the Theory of Folktales by Vladimir Propp

Stories have been told since before humans could speak, even without watching television one could have an idea about narrative (storylines). Propp studied folktales to see what they had in common and analysed the way they were constructed.

Propp defines eight character roles (a pity if you think you've got an original one), basing his theories on the age old stories of ordinary folk such as villains, heroes and princesses:

The eight character roles are as follows:

- The villain.

- The hero.

- The donor (who provides an object with magic properties).

- The helper (partner).

- The princess (obviously).

- The father (rewards the hero).

- The dispatcher (sends the hero on his way).

- The false hero (the jilted lover perhaps).

Obviously, TV cop dramas and Hollywood blockbusters don't necessarily have fairy princesses, heroes and villains – or do they? Start looking.

The Balancing Act – or the Theory of Equilibrium by Tzvetan Todorov

Todorov states that stories start with an 'equilibrium', an assumption about the balance of action within the story, while its disruption is the progress of the story.

But it's not just about the way things are when they start but also about the common ground that underlines that equilibrium, i.e. the cultural assumptions we all agree on. For instance, that a 'normal' family has heterosexual parentage and 2.4 children.

Possibly the 'equilibrium' is informed by the 'backstory': in other words, the story about the main characters that is never told. Their history (i.e. how they got to be where there are at the start), and what and who made them the characters we are now viewing.

Breaking the codes – or Five Theories of Action and Storytelling by Roland Barthes

Roland Barthes has narrowed the action down to five basic codes, even more depressing if you thought you had a great original storyline. The codes are pretty simple:

1) The action or proairetic.

2) The enigma or hermeneutic (interpretation).

3) The semic (signified).

4) The symbolic.

5) The cultural (referential).

When Barthes uses the word 'code' he means it. This is the study of the way in which stories are told with little hints as to what their content is, what the outcome is likely to be and what the characters are like. Stories, in this mode, are more like puzzles, perhaps a puzzle with some missing pieces, and what keeps you interested are the bits that you fill in yourself.

Zeroes and Ones – or How Claude Lévi-Strauss Suggests Stories are Series of Binary Opposites

Conflict, it is said, is the essence of drama. Without the odd argument (frank exchange of views) you can't have drama. Whilst some may query this Lévi-Strauss suggests that stories are largely made up of binary oppositions:

Mythemes – the smallest unit of a story.

Time narrative – a chronological story; a typical linear narrative told in time.

Timeless narrative – a meaning transmitted without the need for time for example we understand the meaning of the idiom looks can kill.

In essence narrative works with a balance of opposition:

Good   Evil

Male   Female

Young   Old

There are many more; think of a few in **The Usual Suspects**.

Classroom Worksheets

Hunt the Protagonist

Who is the protagonist of **The Usual Suspects**?

- Is it Dean Keaton who appears to be an innocent party in the line up? Except that as we learn more about him it seems he is a corrupt cop with a murderous past.

- Is it Verbal Kint who narrates the story and offers us his version of events as he observed and participated in them? Except that he may also be the antagonist Keyser Soze

- Is Dave Kujan, the law enforcement officer whose task it is to solve the puzzle? In a conventional narrative he would be a contender for protagonist.

Nominations for protagonist in **The Usual Suspects**

Who do you think is the protagonist in this film, and why and what narrative and genre conventions qualify your candidate for the title protagonist?

Dean Keaton:

- Role in the story.

- Genre conventions.

- Narrative purpose.

Verbal Kint:

- Role in the story.

- Genre conventions.

- Narrative purpose.

Dave Kujan:

- Role in the story.

- Genre conventions.

- Narrative purpose.

Map the Plot

TASK

Try mapping the plot according to one of the narrative theories – take the idea of binary and attempt to see how it works in the film

Choose one of the following tasks:

1. Map the plot through the use of chronological storyboard pictures of crucial moments in the film.

2. Examine the characters according to the ideas of character role suggested by Todorov.

3. Describe how Barthes' codes can be evidenced in the film.

Sight and Sound

There is no doubt that *The Usual Suspects* owes its considerable success to a variety of factors, not least its script, visual skill, cinematography, director and its cast, but the use of sound and music in the film is perhaps a little credited aspect of that contribution. It is a credit to the largely untried editor of the film, John Ottman, who was also the composer of the music, that the film picked up three awards and nominations for editing and music. When the music and sound are mixed effectively it is barely noticeable as an augmentation of the images, even if it dominates the senses. When sound and image clash all you can think is 'Who the hell is playing that violin?' This was not the case in *The Usual Suspects*. The film collected some prestigious awards for its editing:

- **Science Fiction, Fantasy & Horror Films, USA 1996: The Saturn Award for Best Music.**

- **American Cinema Editors, USA 1996: Eddie Best Cinema Editing (Nominated).**

- **BAFTA, UK 1996: Best Editing.**

The fact that, on this occasion, the music was written by the film's editor, perhaps made the film more compelling since it was one man's vision of sight and sound. Both *Desperado* (1995) and *Once Upon A Time In Mexico* (2003), and more recently the very successful *Sin City* (2005), include tight editing and sound. Robert Rodriguez writes, directs, edits and is the cinematographer for the latter film as well as writing some of the music: an individual vision can make for an individual film. In the absence of one man who controls the whole structure and devises the film, a group of friends with the same vision can also deliver an individual piece. John Ottman met Bryan Singer at USC, Singer also met Kenneth Kokin (a producer on the film) and with high school friend Christopher McQuarrie the team was complete.

Matt Damon and Ben Affleck are a famous team created from a childhood friendship. They won the Oscar for the Best Screenplay with *Good Will Hunting* (1997, dir. Gus Van Sant), that they both performed in and wrote. I always recommend that classmates look around, perhaps the winning team is there.

Perhaps a more neglected aspect of study both in terms of a subject and in terms of a prospective career is the role of the editor and the selection and use of sound and music in films. There is a severe shortage of sound engineers in the business of media. Sound engineering is not considered to be a glamorous area of the profession, particularly by the young, but a good sound engineer and a brilliant editor can compliment or damage a film. There is a precedent for great directors keeping the same cinematographers and film editors. Martin Scorsese works exclusively with Thelma Schoonmaker: Scorsese is her film partner, while Michael Powell, a great British director most famous for the film starring David Niven, *A Matter of Life and Death* (1946), was her husband.

Music

Music is rarely, if ever, credited as either the reason for the success of a film or the cause of its downfall. However, film themes and musical moments are easily remembered and often repeated. Who can forget Peter O'Toole standing atop the train to the sweeping themes of *Lawrence of Arabia* (1962, dir. David Lean)? Could one imagine *The Third Man* without the Harry Lime theme? Would the James Bond films or the *Mission: Impossible* (1996, dir. Brian De Palma) have had the impact that they did without their famous and dramatic scores? Would *Jaws* and *Psycho* be so scary without the resonance of their frightening music?

However, for a long time film companies failed to recognise the impact of music in film both on the product and as commercial potential. In the early 1970s, thousands of music-related materials were destroyed to free up the studio lots' limited storage facilities. At the time there did not appear to be any commercial use for a big back catalogue. Who would want to see old films in the cinema? There would be a niche market for fans of Hitchcock or noir. Once in a while a good soundtrack (usually of a musical) carried on

NOTES:

selling on vinyl, but the commercial viability of old films was limited and the studios were running out of storage. They dumped huge stocks of film and film related artifacts including the music.

In one particularly enthusiastic spring clean Metro-Goldwyn-Mayer actually threw away its collection of classic film music manuscripts, orchestrations, sketches and original recordings into a landfill. Anyone who works in the music business knows that performing the music is not necessarily the way to make money, writing and publishing are, and dumping scores is akin to throwing money away. However, this compelled a group of motivated musicians and friends to meet and form the Music and Film Society (http://www.filmmusicsociety.org/). This group encourages audiences and institutions to view the production of music for film as a cultural and artistic contribution as well as a commercial prospect and film necessity. It encourages the study of film music and it has set up archives, forums and a journal ('*The Cue Sheet*'). The intention is to have film music re-established as an integral part of a film's existence. It may still be that it is not credited sufficiently as part either of the film's success or its failure but music is here to stay.

The Return of Music

It is not that music has never been important in the construction of a film. Obviously there was once a time when music was the *only* sound there was that accompanied a film. Those were the improvised tunes of the pianist at the exhibition house. Once sound could be incorporated into a film, music and its influence became an integral part of the audio code of almost every film. The pundits who have observed the development of film music suggest that the advent of John Williams' score for *Star Wars* in 1977 moved the presence of film music from the undertones of the narrative to the commercial realities of orchestral music.

Commercial Music

Music for money, independent from the film, divides into three distinct packages:

Soundtrack

This is perhaps the oldest and most trusted form of film music. The soundtrack consists of the tracks used in the film. If the film is a musical then the songs are included on CD. In the very old days it used to be possible to buy versions of the soundtrack, sung by artists other than those on the film, quite often from the stage version of the musical.

More recently soundtracks have consisted of compilations of the music featured in a film. Anything from films like *Footloose* (1984, dir. Herbert Ross), a dance movie that might be expected to feature music tracks, through the deliberate use of nostalgia of music to augment the atmosphere, to films that appear to have no reason to market music, such as *Fahrenheit 9/11* (2004) in which Michael Moore used popular music to augment mood, humour and a political point.

Score

This is the music that accompanies the film. The soundtrack should not be mixed up with the score, although occasionally, the audience is not always clear on which is which. Prince's songs associated with *Batman* (1989, dir. Tim Burton) were famously mistaken with Danny Elfman's (*The Simpsons* theme) score to the *Batman* films. Whereas the soundtrack associates songs with a film some of which may have been written especially for the film, the score underlines the themes. It is an orchestral piece that will overture in the titles, reprise in the film and which is increasingly gaining recognition as a music art form in its own right.

Audio code

The audio code of a film is not merely constructed in its music. The way sound and music are used offers codes to the audience as to the atmosphere of a film. Obvious audio codes in music include the ticking of a clock to build up tension, or the use of dramatic orchestral intervention to indicate the presence of antagonists. A dated version of this code can be seen in Hitchcock's *North by Northwest*, on the first arrival of the kidnappers at Roger Thornhill's

NOTES:

club. If the audience was not aware his kidnappers were bad guys by just looking at their stern faces then the music at that moment leaves them in no doubt.

The use of silence is a trickier form of audio code. Everybody is familiar with the cliché 'It's quiet, too quiet'. This is presumably a reference to the idea that animals and birds go silent in nature when danger approaches. The use of silence can be effective. Few who have seen it will forget the moment in *Don't Look Now* (1973, dir. Nicolas Roeg), starring Donald Sutherland and Julie Christie, where the character played by Sutherland is balanced precariously on a scaffolding plank, inspecting the frescos on the wall of a church. The scene goes silent, the camera takes a wide angled shot and, in slow motion, a plank from the scaffold begins, silently, to fall. The sound only cuts back in as the plank hits the window dislodging Sutherland, leaving him dangling. The impact of the scene is magnified but what is almost the memory of seeing the plank fall – the lack of sound means the interpretation is a little late in coming. The effect is a magnification of the feeling of extreme danger, a feeling that does not let up in the film. (Like *The Usual Suspects*, *Don't Look Now* offers a completely unexpected twist.)

Diegetic Sound
In fact the use of silence and then sound in *Don't Look Now* indicates the use of diegetic sound. In other words sounds that are recorded on location or that should come from the location. A conversation may be dubbed over by actors in studio later, but the intention is to provide sound that should or does come from the location. Another term for it that might be easier to understand is actual sound.

Don't Look Now not only used silence as an audio code but it used diegetic sound extremely successfully. As the character played by Donald Sutherland wanders the streets of Venice, pursuing an unknown and mysterious figure, the sounds of Venice echo around him. Footsteps fade up and down. The sounds are directionless

and the viewer never sees the owner. Somewhere a shutter is closed and people call to each other across the canals and paths. Voices carry on conversations behind closed doors and all the time the viewer hears the water lapping against the walls. Venice, of course, has no cars and so the intensity of the diegetic sound is increased by the clarity of silence. The atmosphere is tense and eerie, and it becomes increasingly threatening as the film reaches its climax.

Non-diegetic Sound
Non-diegetic sound is sometimes defined as commentary sound (as opposed to actual sound). This does not mean that it applies only to narrative commentaries spoken over a film story; non-diegetic sound is simply that sound that would not come from the location. It is the sweeping musical score. It is the voice-over or the narrative; the commentary that the music offers and, in fact, musicians divide the use of music into various individual functions.

Source Sound
Source sound is the musical equivalent of diegetic sound. If a scene is filmed in a disco then the music that would emanate from that disco is recorded and dubbed into the scene. It is, to all intents and purposes, diegetic sound, but for editing purposes the source sound and diegetic sound would be recorded on separate tracks, so that conversation filmed for several angles would be cut and re-edited while the source sound is laid underneath it and plays in one linear track just as it would if that conversation were being held in real time.

The Underscore
Mainstream films and most other films will have a score, the music that becomes the theme of the film: everyone knows the *Star Wars* theme and the *Superman* (dir. Richard Donner, 1978) theme (recently revived by none other than John Ottman for Bryan Singer's *Superman Returns* (2006)). The underscore is the music that tells the story, it fulfils the function that the old piano player in the cinema in the silent days once did. The underscore tells you when to be afraid, when

NOTES:

love is in the air, when the excitement is increasing or when the hero has won the day. It is the music that provides the audio code, which augments the mood, and it can help a film succeed or even fail. As an example of the latter, musicians point to the film *The Rock* (1996, dir. Michael Bay), scored by several people including Nick Glennie-Smith and Hans Zimmer, and starring Sean Connery and Nicholas Cage. The film is straight-forward romp through the world of conspiracy and weapons of mass destruction. Not much wrong with the formula of the story, but an article in Film Score Monthly by Yair Oppenheim[15] states that the underscore was too heavy handed. The music continues at a tremendous pace, loud, exciting and tense throughout. As a consequence the audience do not know when to be afraid, excited or tense. The result is ironically a less intense film than intended; in fact, a less well told story.

My own personal example is the difference between the music and use of sound contained in the film *The Perfect Storm* (2000, dir. Wolfgang Peterson), scored by James Horner, and the film *Master and Commander* (2003, dir. Peter Weir), original music by Iva Davies, Christopher Gordon, Richard Tognetti. Both films feature the battle of man against nature, the howling winds and wild waters of the high seas. The internet build up to the film *The Perfect Storm* featured the screaming wind of a storm on the Grand Banks; it literally does sound like a voice, but in the film, the sound is drowned out by the music, perhaps precisely as a device to lessen the impact of what is, in essence, a very sad film. In *Master and Commander*, as the ship rounds Cape Horn, the full force of the sound of the storm is unleashed on the audience. My personal feeling is that the impact of the story is augmented by the sound of the storm, but then *Master and Commander* is historical fiction as opposed to contemporary drama; the music may have been fulfilling the purpose of the film-makers precisely. Whatever the personal preference for music in film, the underscore is part of the storytelling process.

The Temp Score

The temp score is the music accompanying a film for its initial showing. The film is shown to focus the audience at test screenings for comment; sometimes after these viewings audiences comment on the story, the outlines and the characters, and changes can be made according to audience response and the reaction of the network executives to that response. In a showing of the first version of *Logan's Run* (1976, dir. Michael Anderson) the temp score indicated not only the science fiction story being told but a love story also, and so the emphasis of music, script and publicity were changed. At the test screening of *The Usual Suspects* the executives informed Bryan Singer and John Ottman that they had thought that the score would have been more hip, younger. Director and composer agreed that that was precisely *not* what they had wanted; the score of *The Usual Suspects* has an epic nature that hints at the superhero genre, most particularly when the audience is given an establishing shot of a skyscraper in which the opposing parties conspire to murder each other as the music rises and swells to epic connotations as if some superhero were about to appear atop the building. This hints at the idea that the story of Keyser Soze is more than just the story of a petty criminal with a nasty mind, but a work of evil that over powers all that it touches. It is perhaps not a surprise that John Ottman was awarded the Science Fiction, Fantasy & Horror Films, USA 1996, Saturn Award for Best Music.

Synergy

Synergy is that process by which two products will point to each other, usually by using an aspect of each other in their own product. One of the easiest examples of synergy to use is the relationship of music and song to film. Almost as a matter of course nowadays a major film showcases a song that is attached to the film in some way, sometimes only in the end titles, sometimes as part of the score. The musician or musicians in turn produce a music video for play on all the major music TV channels that includes clips of the film, either in some parallel manner that combines both artists and film. Whitney

NOTES:

15. Yair Oppenhem, '*The Functions in Film Music*', article in http://www.filmscoremonthly.com/features/functions.asp.

Sight and Sound

Houston was both star of the film *The Bodyguard* (1992, dir. Mick Jackson) and its music video of her rendition of 'I Will Always Love You' sung to a smoldering Kevin Costner. It was a Kevin Costner film (*Robin Hood: Prince of Thieves*, 1991, dir. Kevin Reynolds) that kept Bryan Adams' song 'Everything I do' at the top of the UK charts for 16 weeks and in both cases the film itself benefits from what is, in effect, free advertising. However, even as early as 1959, producers were becoming aware of the power of music to sell a film. The ballad 'Do Not Forget Me Oh My Darling' (Tiomkin), the central song and theme of the film *High Noon* (1952, dir. Fred Zimmerman), had an impressive impact on the film's finances, an impact that was not lost on network executives as they commissioned new films.

However, the process of linking a film with a popular song is fraught with a few risks. As John Ottman, composer and editor of *The Usual Suspects* suggests, a song that may have given you 'goose bumps' in 1998 may not have the same effect in 2008, but by then the film is inextricably linked with the song. Who can think of *Titanic* without the Celine Dion song 'My Heart Will Go On', 'combined with the abiding of image of Di Caprio and Winslet set astride the prow of the ship? In time both song and image become a cliché that audiences might very well perceive as embarrassing. Ottman makes the point that associating a film with a high fashion song is likely to date the film in time. Unless the music is integral to the function of the drama or the story, a quickly written pop song, connected to an up and coming, or even an established band, is likely to associate the film with the fortunes of that band or the fashion of that sound.

The Usual Sounds

The Usual Suspects does use sound and music like any other film. However, some aspects of the use of sound and music make it more exceptional. The main role of the film editor is to edit together the images with sound, rather than edit the sound itself. In addition John Ottman's role as composer as well as editor puts in him in a unique position within the film to visualise the way sound works with narrative. The editor must work with the director, the storyboards and with the sound provided but it was Ottman's idea to include the laughter of the actors in the line up shot, because however unrehearsed, however much those scenes were film of the actors mucking about, in the end the narrative was of the characters giggling in the line up and nothing indicated better the bonding of the men with each other and with the audience than their laughter[16] (for the full story check out the DVD extras). As editor it was Ottman who put together the false narrative offered by Dave Kujan about the identity of Dean Keaton and the tight use of sound without picture at the end of the film adds to the mystery of Keyser Soze.

Audio Code

Whilst Bryan Singer provided Ottman with images that enabled him to edit the film visually, Ottman's use of the audio code was masterful in that not only did he use audio codes but he also knew when *not* to use them. Throughout the film the interview scenes are largely devoid of music. If they were to have added music then they may well have added clues and the identity and purpose of Verbal Kint would have been revealed. It was very important to the film-makers that Kevin Spacey did not telegraph the end; it was also important that the music did not either.

However, Ottman does use audio and the audio code. Look at the analysis below and listen to how he tells the story with sound.

Sight

It would be inappropriate, however, to emphasise the sound as the only means to a reading of the images. The representation of vision combined with good sound is what combines audio code and visual conventions into a whole package of semiotics and sound that gives us the language of atmosphere and story. *The Usual Suspects* is a particularly economic story, it is told in 102 minutes, less than two hours, so every word, every image and every sound has to count towards the piece as a whole; nowhere is this more evident than in the opening sequence. Textual analysis of

NOTES:

16. DVD Extra: *Deposing The Suspects*.

this sequence on image and semiotics alone is an interesting and effective method of understanding the style and genre of this story, but combined with the sound, some of the audio codes hint at the layers of meaning to come.

Two Minute Textual Analysis: Image and Audio

00:02:16
Keaton (hereafter known as the smoker – as at first sight we do not know who he is) lights a cigarette.

The music of the preceding sequence has accompanied the slow panning of the camera across the reflections on dark water at night. The credits are run and the music waves up and down with the hint of sinister low notes as we get the business of the credits done.

Extreme Close Up (ECU) 00:02:16
ECU on a book of matches as they all light, the owner does not care that he uses all his matches. This in itself signifies an ending. The fire is in the viewer's face, we get much closer to the matches than we would ever normally dare – perhaps enough to make us flinch.

The only sound we hear is the diegetic sound of the matches being lit.

Cut to Mid Shot 00:02:19
Now we see the owner of the matches, he appears to be lit only by the light of the matches as he lights his cigarette. He is sitting on the ground legs splayed, we know by his body language something is wrong. Some of us may also know that it is a convention for the condemned man to smoke a last cigarette before he is shot by the firing squad. The cigarette may indeed be a signifier.

Now we can hear sounds we cannot explain, such as the sound of running water and a slight

dinging; all this is still diegetic sound.

Cut to Mid Shot 00:02:24
This time we see the source of the sound, a barrel is leaking a liquid, it might be water, but already the semiotics, lighting and the act of the smoker in destroying all his matches, plus his demeanour, suggest something more dangerous.

The sound of the water is louder; we cannot hear the bell.

Cut to Wide Shot 00:02:30
The smoker holds the matchbook, still lit, a little away from him and drops it, now we know what the liquid is, we can also see more clearly that he is on a boat.

The sound is still diegetic. Only the images and location sound tell us the story at the moment.

Cut to Close Up 00:02:34
We watch the flames track along the fuel trail.

The sound remains diegetic.

Cut to Mid Shot 00:02:35
The camera stays still at what might be called a rat's eye view as the flame passes along the track at speed, lighting up the face and body of a dead man behind the line of flame.

The sound is minimal, all is deadly quiet.

Cut to Wide Shot 00:02:37
The camera is repositioned still at the low angle as the flame travels back to its source – we all now know what is about to happen. Tension is increased and the enigma is prevalent. What is going to happen when the inevitable happens? Why is the man resigned to it? What led to this? What will happen next?

The camera tracks the flame as it comes directly towards it and us, only to be extinguished by a dubiously yellow stream of liquid.

Sound is diegetic.

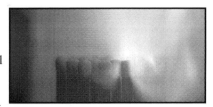

00:02:16

00:02:30

00:02:35

00:02:37

NOTES:

00:02:48

00:02:51

Cut to a Wide Shot 00:02:40
We still get a low view of the extinguishing but from a slightly greater distance, and the camera tracks up to the deck above. The owner of the liquid is above us: powerful, uninhibited, so unafraid, in fact, that he is able to unsheathe his member in the presence of death and fire. It is a universally recognised signal of contempt, potency and territory. It is the act of a winner and the camera, and the viewer, look up, at and to him.

As the camera pans up the music cuts in a low sinister sound at first, the hint of a theme for this character.

Cut to Mid Shot 00:02:48
The smoker is half lit, his expression resigned, signified by the weary smile on his face, his hand hangs by his side, exhausted. He drops his head in defeat.

The music and diegetic sound are now mixed.

Cut to Wide Shot 00:02:51
The figure on the deck above is in silhouette, the low angle is such that we cannot see his head. We do see that he is moving and the camera tracks his progress down the steps. We can barely see him in the darkness.

The low notes of the music above his footsteps moving towards us offer the audio code of fear and danger. His progress is inevitable, his identity unknown, two big signifiers of fear.

Cut to Close Up 00:03:07
We continue with the low angle as the CU of his feet is framed in front of the dead man. It is a signifier of his lack of fear and it connotes his possession of power.

Cut to Mid Shot 00:03:09
The condemned man is smoking, able to look up. His face is never fully lit. The essence of the style of noir is to indicate with light, or lack of it, that dark deeds have taken place and that these are people who inhabit darkness both in deed and character.

As he looks up from his cigarette and makes eye contact with his antagonist, we can hear a bell toll, if we were in any doubt before we know now that he is a condemned man. This is an audio code often used; in almost any Western confrontation, guns drawn uses the sound of a bell tolling.

Cut to Mid Close Up 00:03:18
This is a brief look at the antagonist: only the middle of him is visible as he lights a lighter with ease, with an undamaged hand.

Cut to Close Up 00:03:24
The smoker's face is now almost fully lit. He is also enlightened as to the identity of his antagonist. They speak and the camera stays on the smoker.

The sound now includes all elements: dialogue, music, diegetic sound.

Cut to Close Up 00:03:38
We still look at the middle of the antagonist.

Cut to Close Up 00:03:43
The smoker knows what's about to happen, the CU on his face is level with his position. He is powerless. We see him eye the silhouette of a gun in the front of the frame.

The antagonist speaks in a whisper, he is truly an enigma: we are not supposed to be able to identify him.

Cut to Close Up 00:03:53
We see the antagonist look at his watch, once again we establish his hand is undamaged and that it is past midnight, another significant code. Midnight is the darkest hour, the time that is furthest from the dawn.

Two Shots
The editing speeds up and we cut quickly between the two established shots. The pace of editing is increased and this signifies to us that something is about to happen.

NOTES:

Cut to Point of View (POV) 00:04:07
Now we see the gun as the smoker sees it, in his face. The finger moves to squeeze the trigger.

Cut to Wide Shot 00:04:10/11
We see a shot of the side of the boat. We never see the shots fired, we only hear them as they resound round the boat. There is no response to the sound. Each shot is edited exactly with a sudden change of visual wide shot.

The music rises above the diegetic sound as the lifelessness of the boat is established with several other wide shots of the deserted vessel.

The penultimate shot of this sequence frames a porthole. The music grows more sinister and we stay longer on the shot. If we were observant we might see the blood in the window.

The last shot reminds us of the leaking fuel. It is setting us up for the significance of the next close up.

Cut to Close Up 00:04:27
There is a worm's eye view of the gloved hand as it drops the cigarette. This is a slow motion shot, it gives us time to understand the significance of what is about to happen.

Cut to Mid Shot 00:04:28
The cigarette drops to the fuel track and the antagonist moves away.

The music is now very dramatic and there is a hint of flames in its sound.

Cut to Wide Shot 00:04:30
The camera begins to track very slowly in on a tangle of ropes.

The editing increases pace, the camera cuts through shots of the line of fire, the leaking fuel and the silhouette of the antagonist's escape.

Cut to Long Shot 00:04:33/4
The silhouette of the antagonist as he climbs down reveals the noir semiotics of trench coat

and trilby hat. The silhouette itself reinforces the idea of the archetype – in noir a silhouette is representative of the general evil that men and women do. The individual's identity is lost in the evilness of their acts.

00:04:07

Cut to Mid Shot 00:04:40
Another tracking shot of the line of fire sets up this shot, a mid shot of the palettes and rope as they are lit by the explosion. The camera tracks very slowly in on the ropes.

Cut to Mid Shot 00:04:46
A low angle shot of the fire as it flares up and fills the screen, in a manner reminiscent of the opening of **Blade Runner**.

00:04:46

The music explodes in our ears as the fire leaps up. All this signifies the power of the flames and the idea of this being an ending as well as a beginning, something relevant to the narrative as we shall very soon see.

Cut to Extreme Close Up 00:04:52
The camera continues to track into the ropes, almost on a collision course and as it does so a mid shot of Verbal Kint, lit directly from above, appears in the centre, white like a skeletal apparition.

00:04:52

In the background the diegetic sound of police sirens subdues the music. The music has been reinforcing ideas of drama, even melodrama, huge events, strange goings on. The sound of the siren brings us back to verisimilitude, symbols and signifiers are exchanged for police work and real dialogue, at least for the moment.

NOTES:

Sight and Sound

Table 4.1 Sight and Sound Glossary

Term	Definition
Diegetic	Sound that is recorded and comes from the location.
Non-diegetic	Sound that could not be heard in the location such as narrative and music.
Source sound	Sound that would come from the location such as background music, but which has to be recorded and edited in so that the action and dialogue can be edited separately.
Commentary sound	Sound that offers a commentary – not just a voice narrative but sound that hints at fear, tension, or happiness.
Audio code	Sound that tells the story – the ticking of a clock that hints at a ticking bomb (close in definition to commentary sound – but a bit more immediate).

NOTES:

SOUND ANALYSIS

Scene	Sound
The arrest of Hockney. DVD Chapter 3: Time Code 00:05:22.	The sound of the paint tin mixing has an audio referent – the sound of gunfire. The sound cuts in before the scene begins to allow our imaginations to be fooled into thinking it is gunfire.
The arrest of Fenster. DVD Chapter 3: Time Code 00:05:53.	The sound and visuals are edited such that the music drum beat links with a jump cut in the action. This speeds up the action and tells us all we need to know quickly.
The interrogation of Fenster and Hockney. DVD Chapter 3: Time Code 00:10:14.	Fenster starts to say 'I want my lawyer' and Hockney finishes the sentence. Throughout the interrogation scenes this cutting/linking of the sound across scenes increases pace and makes the narrative more economic.
The burnt body on the boat. DVD Chapter 6: Time Code 00:16:13.	The close up of the charred body on the deck is combined with diegetic sound of the ships horns blowing loudly. The juxtaposition of both sound and image draws our attention, makes us jump, adds drama; in addition, it makes us realise that the sound itself is innocent.
The arrival of Kujan. DVD Chapter 7: Time Code 00:17:18.	As we see the plane arrive we hear Dave Kujan's answerphone message, we know that he is flying into New York (it is an economic way of telling the story).
The New York taxi service. DVD Chapter 11: Time Code 00:29:30.	As Keaton and Kint resolve their differences and decide to join in on the hit on the corrupt policemen's courier service, the ticking of a clock links the two scenes. As the plane flies in it too is edited for sound and vision in the same way as the arrest of Fenster, it increases the pace.
The Korean Friendship Memorial, as the gang meet with Redfoot. DVD Chapter 16: Time Code 00:41:21.	Ottman quite often seems to use music that reflects the location, in this case the Oriental nature of the memorial is reflected in the slightly Oriental instrumentation.
The second heist. DVD Chapter 17: Time Code 00:44:22.	Again Ottman uses diegetic sound and mixes it with the music. As the music builds, the tiny ping of the lift is heard; at first, it sounds like part of the music as it comes in on beat. Only when we see them come out of the lift does it make sense.
The epic score. DVD Chapter 24: Time Code 01:06:20.	The music swells and rises as it does in more epic films. A feeling of epic drama is imposed on the narrative, it hints at a greater sense of threat.
Kujan's narrative. DVD Chapter 30: Time Code 01:29:44–55.	Throughout this narrative Kujan tells the story and his retelling is lip synched with the dialogue on the screen so Verbal says 'certain death' as Kujan does and the Argentinian mouths 'Keyser Soze' in time with Dave Kujan.
Panning through the boat. DVD Chapter 28: Time Code 01:21:41.	As the camera pans through the underbelly of the boat, a real audio code comes into play, the deep chaotic sounds of fear, combined with what sounds like the creaking and scraping of the boat itself.
Last moment. Chapter 32: Time Code 01:38:20-35.	Just as all is revealed we hear Verbal's voice – 'and like that' – we cut to a close up of his face, the screen goes blank and we hear: 'he's gone'.

CLASS TASK

Bring in your favourite moment in film sound, play it, and justify why you think it works and adds to the storytelling.

Teacher's note: This might be a difficult task for large classes to undertake but it could be done in groups with either one group presenting one piece or small groups presenting to one another.

One of the difficult aspects of the study of media for students is being able to understand the relationship between the audience and the film, or the product. Students at GCSE and A Level, even beyond, tend to invest the audience and the producer with infallible judgement. If the audience have rushed in their hordes to see a film then it must be a good film. However, if a film has flopped then it must be awful and not worth the bother. There is little flexibility in the young audience. Unfortunately, they are also the biggest proportion of the cinema going audience (36 per cent of the audience is between 15 and 35).[17] Students will claim that producers and executives make few mistakes and that the direction in which we, as the audience have been led, is the correct course. They tend also to assume the autonomy of the film-maker and the director: films are conceived, made and distributed with little interference from the bank or the executives. Being able to understand the concept of pitching a movie is only half the battle in understanding the workings of the film industry. The most autonomous film is likely to be the cheapest of films. Bryan Singer himself ascribes some of the success of *The Usual Suspects* to the fact that he was 'young and stupid'.[18] He made the film as if it were a childhood project and he was on the set with his friends. Everything then had to be the way he wanted it and there were no accountants to interfere with his vision, although that was partly because, on occasion, there was no money either.

How then does a film ever get made, especially if it does not have the backing of a huge studio and a mass of investors?

Building a Film

The Idea

One idea is usually not enough. At least two friends of mine have tried to pitch ideas to a Hollywood producer, both have struggled with the process because, instead of being allowed to pitch one idea in detail they have had to come up with 20 or so ideas, each of which are judged within seconds of the pitch. Objections such as 'done that before', 'too expensive' and 'too political' are fired at the ideas, detailed judgement rarely seems to come into it.

The idea for *The Usual Suspects*, came up while Christopher McQuarrie, the writer, was standing in the queue for another film at the Sundance Festival (of which more later in this chapter). He was familiar with the phrase 'the usual suspects' and knew the connotations that it had. A magazine article on the subject set him thinking and pretty soon he saw the possibilities of doing a film about five guys who met in a line up. He speculated on the idea, came up with an idea for a poster and left it that.

It was a 'back of an envelope' comment that was remembered by Bryan Singer for later use.

Writer

In this instance the writer and the ideas man were one and the same, although that is not always the case. Screenplays are written, read and handed round to other more expert screenwriters to be rewritten, adapted and altered. There are a great many screenwriters in Hollywood who make a living from writing screenplays but who never see their scripts filmed. Bryan Singer had worked with Christopher on *Public Access*, so when he was approached to come up with some more ideas, he went back to his writer and asked for a pitch and treatment. On the basis that they already a poster, McQuarrie went to work and produced a pitch and three pages of treatment in three days.

The Pitch

In fact, neither Christopher McQuarrie nor Bryan Singer took their idea any further on their own. Their first film *Public Access* had done well (it shared The Grand Jury Prize at Sundance), but one good film does not a career make, McQuarrie was still working as an office boy in a legal firm. They had yet to pitch their idea.

NOTES:

17. www.pearlanddean.com/marketdata/audience.html.
18. DVD Feature, Doin' Time with *The Usual Suspects*.

Film, Audience and Product

No doubt linguists would tell you that the phrase 'the pitch' comes from baseball – you pitch or throw the ball to your opponent who must hit it for a home run. It is your offering to the player to do with as he/she must. One of the most biting portrayals of the pitching process is at the beginning of Robert Altman's film *The Player* (1992). The arrogant and smooth film executive played by Tim Robbins listens to a pair of film-makers who are desperately trying to pitch their movie ideas. Each time he makes a comment they adapt their idea to include the cast, concepts and plot twists that the executive is likely to accept. His motivation is not art or story but money and audience. No player in this game enters the arena with only one idea and it is to the credit of Bryan Singer and his previous film that he was able, with Christopher McQuarrie, to pitch and carry through one idea. It is part of what makes *The Usual Suspects* unusual. However, that process was only made possible by the intervention of Robert Jones, a former acquisitions manager who saw their potential and championed it to investors and studios.

The Treatment

They had already come up with the poster and the tagline 'All of you can go to hell'. They had a poster so they needed a treatment. It is hard to describe the creation of the pitch without describing one of the major punchlines of the film, but as McQuarrie's day job was office work in a law firm, in the office he found the names and ideas for the first script and proposal for *The Usual Suspects* – everything from the barber shop quartet in Skokie, Illinois to the names of Verbal Kint and Keyser Soze.

The treatment is the written part of the pitch. Straczynski[19] (whose book 'The Complete Book of Scriptwriting' is still the definitive guide for most TV and, to some extent, film scriptwriters) advises a limited written treatment: too many paragraphs and the pitcher will get tangled up in plot lines, characters and nuances; the executives will get bored and lose interest. In the case of *The Usual Suspects*, Christopher McQuarrie put together a script and treatment in double quick

time and he, Singer and producer Robert Jones took it to 130 studios, producers, agents and individuals – all of whom turned it down. Objections included: too much dialogue, not enough action, too confusing, unknown writer, inexperienced director, the bad guy gets away with it and everybody dies. The objections that the studios raised had to do with genre, audience expectations and investment.

Successful films, in the view of many studio 'players', have attributes that are demonstrable in other films. They are High Concept movies, with formulaic plots, A-list actors, plenty of action, romance and computer graphics (CGI). Gabriel Byrne defines the executive produced movie as the Mac Movie,[20] a burger and bun approach to movie-making, an approach that is formulaic, easy and quick to consume and so make a profit. *The Usual Suspects* was none of these and so, as far as the studios were concerned, it was doomed to failure.

A Piece of Talent

An additional plus to your movie, if you have a script and treatment and you are ready to make a pitch, is to have a piece of talent. This is an interested actor, preferably someone with a reputation. The bigger the reputation, the more likely it is that your movie will get made. The pitch can first be made either to the actor or the actor's agent through the script. Actors may receive scripts from studios who want them to contract to their film, or from directors who want their presence in a film, or they may acquire scripts themselves in the hope of getting a script made. If the actor is an A-list star they are an 'opener' which means that they can open a movie, this means that people will go and see the film because of the actor. It does not matter whether Robert De Niro is a cop, a killer or a comedy act, followers of De Niro will go to see him in any role. He can open a movie (although they are rarely blockbusters). Quite often actors will use this status to get something made that would otherwise never make it to the screen. Clint Eastwood has long since had his own production company, Malpaso Productions, that has made films featuring a strong script, often

---

NOTES:

19. J. Michael Straczynski, *The Complete Book of Scriptwriting*, (London: Titan, 1987).

20. Byrne, *Nothing is What it Seems: The Making of The Usual Suspects*, TV (1998), prod. Louis Heaton.

not suited to any particular genre, nor to some of the generic roles that he has been used to playing, but starring himself in different roles. Malpaso Productions has taken him as a director, through anything from his first effort *Play Misty For Me* (1971) which featured the man as victim, through *White Hunter, Black Heart* (1990), *Unforgiven*, *The Bridges of Madison County* (1995), *Mystic River* (2003) and *Million Dollar Baby* (2004). Other actor/directors such as Mel Gibson (ICON Productions) have followed that lead – how else could a violent portrayal of the passion of Christ get made and exhibited in Aramaic?

Bryan Singer had also formed his own production company Bad Hat Harry which is now producing America's biggest selling TV series about a maverick doctor, *House*, starring Hugh Laurie in an American role. Back in 1995, as well as having set up his own production company, Bryan Singer had a 'piece of talent', although this actor was not, as yet an A-list, opener. He was Kevin Spacey, an admirer of *Public Access*, a recent star in the film *Swimming with Sharks* (1994, dir. George Huang) (along with Benicio del Toro – and a must see film for any student of the media). Spacey was a solid theatre actor with good reputation. He was on the verge of stardom but he was not yet a household name. He was their piece of talent. In that sense Spacey probably exemplified the meaning of the idiom 'piece of talent' in that he did possess talent rather than fame. Spacey admired *Public Access* and was instrumental in remaining a supporter of *The Usual Suspects* and in persuading a better known piece of talent Gabriel Byrne to finally agree to his role in the film. Both Robert De Niro and Christopher Walken who Bryan Singer did try for, turned it down.[21]

For Bryan Singer, finding a cast that would fit together well was a tough gig. Once you have a piece of talent they usually want to work with people less well known than themselves, well known actors hesitate to act with others who may upstage them, or who may have a more pivotal role than they have. Whilst the portrayal of a character in the film might seem to be the most important consideration when casting a movie, if an actor makes a wrong decision about a role, years of careful strategy with regard to building a career, along with the audience itself. The casting of *The Usual Suspects* was so sensitive that along with its many other accolades, the casting agent was also given an award. For the most part Bryan Singer knew what he wanted and found actors, or persuaded actors that they were right for the role. In the end, even Gabriel Byrne capitulated, on the basis of a short shooting time, in his home at the time of LA. Some of this cast was decided on along with the script and some of it came with the money, but in the short term the job was to find the money.

Acquisitions

In the case of McQuarrie and Singer they had some kudos from the critical success of *Public Access*. Kevin Spacey saw the film; Robert Jones, formerly in acquisitions, saw the film. *Public Access* needed only to be seen by those two men before it had a chance of serving its successor well. Phone calls were made and Christopher McQuarrie was asked to make good on his cinema queue idea.

Money

The idea might be the most important aspect of the film, without it there is no film, but as soon as the idea and, in this case, the poster is decided the deal must be done. Somehow the idea must be connected to its audience and none of this can be done without money. The process for film and TV is similar. In both processes there is a lot of money involved. It is not a simple matter of pencil and paper, typewriter and ribbon or keyboard and screen. Film is a huge undertaking, it requires people, money and equipment. Even *The Blair Witch Project* (1999, dir. Daniel Myrick & Eduardo Sánchez) cost $35,000 and that's without a set, major props, stars or even good cameras and lighting. In order for a film to get made it must get financial backing. The pitch is the first step towards that process and a part of the pitch is the treatment.

NOTES:

21. www.imdb.com, *The Usual Suspects* – Trivia.

Film, Audience and Product

In the case of *The Usual Suspects* the money came from a variety of sources and was linked to ownership. On one particular day they lost 35 per cent of their funding and could only raise more money when they managed to claw back some of the copyright and offer a better deal to another investor.

Publicity
The Importance of Being Noticed

Most audiences are aware of the part played by awards in the marketing and success of a film or a book. The Oscars dominate the annual film circuit, but the lead up to the Oscars includes a myriad of festivals, premiers and publicity that are designed, first and foremost, to bring a film to the attention of its audience and then to extend that attention to maximum sales and box office returns. A film that becomes an Oscar nominee or winner often comes before the Academy with a collection of awards already attached to it. The Golden Globes is a prestigious set of awards in the entertainment business given by The Hollywood Foreign Press Association, an association of international journalists based in Southern California, whose purpose it is to foster better cultural relations between America and the rest of the world. There is the Palme d'Or, the most prestigious prize from the Cannes Film Festival, or the Grand Jury Prize from Sundance, the Critics Award from those or other festivals and a variety of best actor or best director awards from a variety of professional associations involved in the media. The more of these that a film can pick up, the more likely they are to do well at the box office

Awards are important because of the recognition that they offer to the film-maker. When actors, directors, writers and others receive their awards, for them personally it is an affirmation of their talent. It is a vindication of their sacrifice and the sacrifices of others as they struggle to steer their project through the system to the screen. However, for the producers, the value of an award goes beyond recognition of personal achievement, it sells a film. Just like the effect of the Booker Prize

on an author's sales of their books, films are affirmed by awards and sales at the box office go up. Clever producers and companies angle their release dates, their publicity and their posters at the Oscars. *The English Patient* (1996, dir. Anthony Minghella), for instance, was a delightful atmospheric film starring slightly known English actors and produced by Saul Zaentz, based, of course, on a Booker Prize-winning novel by Michael Ondaatje. They released it close to the Oscar nominations, gambling that a recent film would attract nominations. It did, they reprinted posters and ran a campaign, highlighting its nominated status while it was still open at the box office. When it won, they produced more posters, more publicity and finally a fashion tie-in to reproduce the clothes. This did not happen to Saul Zaentz's previous film *At Play in the Fields of the Lord* (1995, dir. Hector Babenco). It featured a strong cast (John Lithgow, Tom Berenger, Aidan Quinn, Daryl Hannah and Kathy Bates), a very strong script – and no success. If you get a chance, get yourself a big pot of coffee and the DVD; it is worth a look. However, the most important function of most festivals is for a film to attract the attention of the distributors and the audience in the first place. At their most fundamental level festivals provide a screen and the opportunity for an audience to see the film.

Alternative and Mainstream

One of the concepts that young media students find it hardest to come to grips with is the idea that mainstream films are not necessarily 'the be all and the end all' of quality. The fact that a film can grab an audience of millions and make a huge amount of money is not the only pointer to its merit. However, teenagers tend to discount very readily the past and the alternative, until, that is, they want to make their own film and get it marketed.

Festivals: Alternative
The Sundance Festival

One of the most successful independent film festivals in recent years has been the Sundance

NOTES:

Film Festival. It is independent because its initial purpose was to showcase films made by film-makers who raised their own finance and made films that did not necessarily fit the conventions of the mainstream Hollywood movie. Films are submitted, viewed by committee and accepted or rejected for screening at the annual festival which takes place in Park City, Utah in January at the height of the ski season.

The Sundance Festival has not always been called that. It started as the U.S. Film Festival in 1978 in Salt Lake City, although its prime motivation was the same and that was to showcase movies made outside of the standard studio system. The mythology of the festival suggests that film director Sydney Pollack suggested the move to Park City and the time of year, his point being that then it would be the only film festival to be held at that time of year and thus it would have no competitors. In parallel, in 1981, local resident Robert Redford, founded the Sundance Institute. This was a small institution made up of friends and colleagues and it was intended to encourage and train hopeful new screenwriters. A student of the media needs to know that the reason for the name has its source in the history of Robert Redford's career. One of his most famous roles was as the Sundance Kid, opposite Paul Newman as Butch Cassidy in the film detailing the possible biography of *Butch Cassidy and The Sundance Kid* (1969, dir. George Roy Hill).

From 1981 to 1995 the U.S. Film Festival and the Sundance Institute continued to operate in parallel, in 1985 they amalgamated their operation and in 1991 the festival took the name the Sundance Festival. Its setting is not entirely inappropriate, Park City was a Western boom town in the age of the Wild West, growing at great speed and bringing with it all the traditions of the Wild West and its myths. Now skiers and film-makers mix on the pavements in January and, its population increases from 6,000 to 20,000 in that one week of the festival. High-heeled Hollywood women stagger along the pavements alongside ski booted sports men and cynical locals.

'When I came to Sundance, I was a wage slave. And then, twenty-four hours later, I had a filmmaking career,' quotes Kevin Smith.[22]

Kevin Smith will be best known to students as Silent Bob, a character he created in the film *Clerks* (1994); a film he both wrote and directed. His was not the only life changed. Steven Soderbergh's *sex, lies and videotape* (1989) won the audience award at Sundance and went on to win the Palme d'Or at Cannes. *The Blair Witch Project*, made for $35,000, sold to distributors for just over one million dollars after a midnight screening at Sundance, it went on to make $140,000, 000 – not bad for a little movie shown at midnight.

Needless to say the Sundance Festival has become a victim of its own success; for each category in the competition which screens 16 films, hundreds are submitted.

Such success has its critics. Now Sundance has to turn films down and with the extent of talent applying to the festival it is becoming harder and harder to suggest that those rejected are not worthy of a place at the festival. As with all festivals, alternatives and fringe festivals abound: Slamdance showcases rejected films, No Dance shows DVD projected films and SlamDunk showcased Nick Broomfield's Sundance rejected *Kurt and Courtney* (1998). In Britain, the aptly titled Raindance Festival plans to make its own progress in showcasing British films with the hope of wider distribution or merely recognition for their quality.

Sundance is the refuge of the young: 57 per cent of attendees are between 18 and 35 years old, and while they might be wedded to their art, very few of them would mind the big money success offered by Hollywood. It is the Sundance Festival's intention to reward for artistic merit rather than commercial success; however, one of the problems that it faces is that once having been rewarded for merit, commercial, mainstream success is almost inevitable. Kenneth Turan in his book 'Sundance to Sarajevo',

NOTES:

22. Kevin Smith in Kenneth Turan, *Sundance to Sarajevo: Film Festivals and the World They Made* (Berkeley: University of California, 2003), p.31.

suggests that for the Sundance Festival the turning point came when, in 1996, they showcased the film *Shine* (1996, dir. Scott Hickson), starring Geoffrey Rush as the pianist David Helfgott. It was, technically an independent film, but it also contained the conventions of an old-fashioned Hollywood movie. It went on to win seven Oscar nominations. The relationship between Sundance and the mainstream was cemented.

Sundance, however, still adheres to its philosophy of the alternative: 'Despite the number of successful films that have debuted at Sundance, it's difficult to escape the feeling that the competition selection process has an unmistakable anti-commercial bias. This may sound noble and honorable, but in reality it's a counterproductive exercise in artistic elitism that does the independent movement no good at all.'[23] In 1995 the year before *Shine*, the Grand Jury Prize did *not* go to *The Usual Suspects*, the jury were divided over a variety of rarified choices. The relationship between Hollywood and its alternative remains fraught: who can remember what happened to the choice of that year, *The Brothers McMullen* (1996, dir. Edward Burns)? But *The Usual Suspects* went on to win two Oscars and it went via Cannes.

Festivals: Mainstream
Cannes

By the time Singer and McQuarrie got to Cannes, news of their film had gone before them. The red carpet was rolled out, the interview schedule extended by days and the actors and crew lauded and praised in the usual Hollywood style until, at last, Kevin Pollack (Todd Hockney) was heard to exclaim 'It's a movie, get over it!'

Where the Sundance Festival's initiating and continuing ethos is to offer to film-makers the opportunity to showcase films that do not, necessarily, fit the commercial definition of a successful movie, Cannes is more than happy to showcase the Hollywood style in the chic and slightly decadent setting of the South of France. Cannes awards the Palme d'Or and that is the

film world's most coveted prize after the Oscars. Cannes was a post-war invention. It started in 1946, an affirmation of victory in Europe, a return to the trivial and the decadent. Cannes skipped 1948 and then in 1954 actress Simone Sylva dropped her bikini top in front of Robert Mitchum and glamour, sensationalism and scandal came to town. Cannes embraced it wholeheartedly. In 1959, Cannes started its Marché International du Film (MIF). This established Cannes as a market place, a commercial zone, for the buying and selling of films.

In 1968 the decadence got too much for some and as part of the uprising of students and others against the domination of capitalism, two directors, Jean-Luc Goddard and François Truffaut, got the festival cancelled halfway through. In the next year an alternative festival, Quinzaine des Realisteurs (Directors' Fortnight) was set up and it continues to showcase the more adventurous offerings to the Hollywood canon. Actor Tim Robbins described Cannes as a strange mixture of 'the art of film and the total prostitution of film.'[24] The need to show completed works competes with the impulse to sell and buy not just completed works, but ideas, concepts and talent.

Despite its position as one of the most important festivals on the film calendar, Cannes is a fickle mistress for Hollywood. Like Sundance it can sometimes make inexplicable choices when it comes to accepting films for screening. Pundits cite the screening of Johnny Depp's directorial effort, *The Brave* (1997) as an incomprehensible decision. The film, they say was impossible to sell. Cannes is a competition and being entered for the competition alone is compliment to the film and likely to affirm its success, but in the past films like *Strictly Ballroom* (1992, dir. Baz Luhrmann) and *Trainspotting* (1996, dir. Danny Boyle) have been denied access to the competition. Those who study the form suggest that Cannes favours the known director, the auteur with a good reputation and even if the film is not that great the director will get their chance. This tendency to be unpredictable when it comes to the quality of the films entered in the competition

---

NOTES:

23. Turan, *Sundance to Sarajevo: Film Festivals and the World They Made* (Berkeley: University of California, 2003), p. 46.
24. ibid, p. 21.

has meant that some do not even attempt to enter. Ridley Scott's *Gladiator* (2000) passed on the opportunity to be considered. Cannes is a place where such a film can be relegated to out of competition slots, or a place where it can be booed from the screen. Hollywood studios are not fond of taking such chances. Cannes can finish a movie, and studios do not want to risk the tens of millions of dollars they may have spent on a film disappearing down the drain on the whim of a competition that has narrow ideas about what constitutes a good film.

Festival Round Up

Despite the fact that *The Usual Suspects* received a great reception at the Cannes Film Festival it did not win; but the publicity and the opportunities generated on the beaches at Cannes confirmed its place in the wider competition for money, accolades and awards. It went on to win two Oscars: Best Screenplay for Christopher McQuarrie and Best Supporting Actor for Kevin Spacey. A look at the awards picked up by the film indicates that, in this case, quality, originality and commercialism combined to make a successful film moment for all the participants. The awards are listed in Table 5.1 below.

Marketability

Awards get attention but unless you can distribute the movie, get it out to the audience, the film will not succeed. Festival shelves are loaded with wonderful films that never make it to screen (this is a particular problem for the British film industry).

The biggest issues facing an acquisitions manager or network executive in a film production company are the possibilities for marketing. What *The Usual Suspects* showed was that even a film that might appear not to have marketability could be marketed and could be successful. It did not have any of the usual attributes of an obviously marketable film, no major star, a first time director, an unknown writer, a bleak amoral ending that did not fit with the controlling ideology that crime should not pay and no major special effects.

A network executive preparing to market a film would look for the following:

- Some adherence to a recognised genre (science fiction, thriller, romantic comedy).

- An A-list star or two (Tom Cruise/Julia Roberts).

- A pedigree (directed by Joe Bloggs, his best since *Nightmare in the Classroom*).

- A USP (unique selling point) – a first partnership between stars, new use of CGI, an amazing plot twist.

- CGI.

The Usual Suspects only had one of those attributes and that narrowly – the end is a twist but it is dark. Possibly Gabriel Byrne was sufficiently well known to attract attention but not to 'open' the film. It did have a poster that became iconic, and its USP became the fact that it was precisely *not* any of the things that a network executive would expect to see in a film. It had one more thing that made it saleable – playability.

Playability

An executive can put millions of dollars into marketing a film but if it does not play well to an audience on the night, word of mouth will kill it within a week. Perhaps the most famous loser in the playability game is Kevin Costner whose films *The Postman* (1997) and *Waterworld* (1995) lost a total of $150 million during their theatrical runs.

The Postman – estimated budget $80 million.

Gross as of December 1997 approx $17 million.

Box office losses $63 million.

Waterworld – estimated budget $175 million.

Gross as of September 1995 approx 88 million.

Box office losses $87 million.

While both films had were all the conventions that would make them marketable, including

---

NOTES:

Film, Audience and Product

Kevin Costner, neither film played well with the audience and the list of such films is endless. It would be unfair to suggest that Kevin Costner was the only loser in the film business. Judging what the audience will like is a tricky business and while marketing campaigns, famous names and fabulous stories all help, sometimes the audience just decides it likes the film with no stars and a hand-held camera. It is not even as if the critics and the audience will agree on the quality of a film either. *Titanic* was disdained by the critics but the audience flocked to it; to date it has made over $600 million. The audience is fickle.

The Usual Suspects Results

The Usual Suspects had both marketability and playability although it also had a slow start. It opened in only 42 US cinemas (a huge release will see a film in 3,000 cinemas) on 20 August 1995. It took $645,363 on its first weekend and it was ranked 18th in the weekend charts. In fact that was not a bad start. On 15th September its success merited a wider release, although it only ever went to 876 cinemas and on that weekend it made $3,017,130, 12.9% of its final gross. Word had got around and *The Usual Suspects* stayed in the top 20 then for nearly two months and by the end of October it had made $20,868,504. Not a bad return on 6 weeks filming and a $6 million dollar investment. The total box office gross in the US was in excess of $23 million.[25]

NOTES:

25. Figures from www.boxofficemojo.com.

Table 5.1 Awards for *The Usual Suspects*

Award	Recipient
Academy Awards, USA 1996 Oscar Best Actor in a Supporting Role Best Writing, Screenplay Written Directly for the Screen	Kevin Spacey Christopher McQuarrie
Academy of Science Fiction, Fantasy & Horror Films, USA 1996 Saturn Award Best Music Nominated Saturn Award: Best Director	Best Action/Adventure Film John Ottman Bryan Singer
American Cinema Editors, USA 1996 Nominated Eddie: Best Edited Feature Film	John Ottman
BAFTA, UK 1996 Best Editing Best Film Best Screenplay	John Ottman (USA) Bryan Singer, Michael McDonnell (USA) Christopher McQuarrie (USA)
Boston Society Film Critics Award, USA 1996 Best Supporting Actor	Kevin Spacey
Casting Society of America, 1996 USA Best Casting For a Feature Film	Francine Maisler
Chicago Film Critics Award Best Screenplay Best Supporting Actor	John Ottman Kevin Spacey
Chlotrudis Awards, 1996 Best Supporting Actor	Kevin Spacey
Cesar Awards, France 1996 Best Foreign Film (Meilleur film étranger)	Bryan Singer
Dallas–Fort Worth Critics Associations Awards, USA 1996 Best Supporting Actor	Kevin Spacey
Edgar Allen Poe Awards, USA 1996 Best Motion Picture	Christopher McQuarrie
Empire Awards UK, UK 1996 Best Debut	Bryan Singer
Golden Globes, USA 1996 Nominated Best Performance by an Actor in a Supporting Role in a Motion Picture	Kevin Spacey
Independent Spirit Awards, 1996 Best Screenplay Best Supporting Male Nominated Best Cinematographer	Christopher McQuarrie Benicio del Toro Thomas Newton Sigel
Kinema Junpo Awards, 1996 Readers' Choice Award: Best Foreign Language Film	Bryan Singer
National Board of Review, USA 1995 Best Acting by an Ensemble Best Supporting Actor	Stephen Baldwin, Gabriel Byrne, Benicio del Toro, Kevin Pollack, Kevin Spacey, Chazz Palminteri, Pete Postlethwaite, Suzy Amis, Giancarlo Esposito Kevin Spacey (also for *Se7en*)

Film, Audience and Product

Award	Recipient
New York Film Critics Circle Award, USA 1995 Best Supporting Actor	Kevin Spacey (also for *Se7en*, *Swimming with Sharks*, *Outbreak*)
Sant Jordi Awards, 1996 Best Foreign Actor (Mejor Actor Extranjero)	Chazz Palminteri (also for *A Bronx Tale* and *Bullets Over Broadway*)
Screen Actors Guild Awards, 1996 Nominated Outstanding Performance by a Male Actor in a Supporting Role	Kevin Spacey
Seattle International Film Festival, USA 1995 Golden Space Needle Award: Best Actor Best Director	Kevin Spacey (also for *Swimming with Sharks*) Bryan Singer
Tokyo International Film Festival, 1995 Silver Award	Bryan Singer

Fantasy Festival

TASK

Imagine you have an unlimited budget to create a film festival, how would you go about putting such a festival together; what would be your priorities?

Think through your festival, for example:

- Where would you stage your festival and why that location?

- What categories would you include?

- Would this be a themed festival? Or a particular genre?

- Would you keep it mainstream or showcase independent films?

- How would you encourage new film-making?

- Would you include foreign films?

- Would you include short films?

- What prizes would you offer?

- What support would you try and get from the industry?

- What impact would you hope your festival would have on the industry?

- How would you set about marketing your festival?

Bryan Singer: An Unusual Auteur?

Singer on the set of *The Usual Suspects*

Whose Film is it Anyway?

In France in the 1950s the traditional conventions of film-making were coming under fire. Up until then the idea of film-making was preoccupied with verisimilitude – that is, how to make a film look real. Media and film is a new industry; it started with grainy photographs taken of people who had to stand still for a very long time, hence the occasionally smudged faces and very stern faces. The move from a painted portrait to a photograph, however dingy, represented the real just that little bit more accurately. The still photograph moved on to the moving image. People move, so film aspired to move, although, to begin with the speedy movements and the lack of sound still reminded the audience that they were watching an imitation. Gradually technology and technique combined to imitate the real effectively and until the 1950s the idea that cinema and film might not be realistic was not considered (at least as far as mainstream, mass-market cinema was concerned). Film held up a mirror, a photograph or a moving image that

was simply a reflection of life. However, for some film-makers the idea of making film that was merely a copy seemed unsatisfactory. It seemed that film-makers were capable of more than simple imitation, and focused on creation.

France has always had a strong and individualistic film-making industry. Many French film-makers have achieved international reputations, many more remain successful in France, supporting a tradition of film-making that gives French films their individuality, a counter to the Hollywood conventions, at least in France. However, it was with the French that auteur theory began.

In 1954, François Truffaut wrote an essay called 'Une certaine tendence du cinéma français', published in *'Cahiers du Cinema'*.[26] At the time Truffaut was still a critic; he released his first film (***Une Visite***) in 1955. For most of his career he worked in France, although in 1966 he made a famously disturbing film based on the science fiction writer, Ray Bradbury's, novel 'Fahrenheit 451'. In addition, ***A bout de soufflé*** (1960, dir. Jean Luc Godard), which he wrote, was remade as a Hollywood version, ***Breathless*** starring Richard Gere (1983, dir. Jim McBride). In his essay in 1954 he argued that there was no such thing as a bad movie but bad *directors* and that even the worst movie made by the likes of Jean Renoir or Alfred Hitchcock can still be interesting because of the talent that conceived it, and that talent rests with the director.

The effect of the article in *'Cahiers du Cinema'* was a little like that of the movement of 'the Angry Young Men' in Britain in the late Fifties and early Sixties. It was iconoclastic; the young French film-makers were impatient with the triviality of much film-making, very little reference was made to politics or meaning. The preoccupations of popular film-making were shallow and self-obsessed. Hollywood films portrayed middle class Americans, trying to raise babies, fight wars or murder each other.

Auteur theory is a theory applied to film-making and is more widely taught in Film Studies.

NOTES:

26. www.moviesunlimited.com/truffaut/htm.

It makes the suggestion that the director creates the film. The *politique des auteurs* separated the idea of the author of the original story from the influence of the director. It credited the director with the creation and style of the film. Truffaut and followers of the theory stated that a director's influence could be tracked by the consistent themes and ideas that recurred in their films. It provides a tool that is structuralist in nature, a method by which the audience or critic can identify the recurring themes in a film-maker's career and thereby identify him or her as an auteur. For example Peter Wollen[27] examines the work of John Ford. He identifies similarities in themes and narrative style in **The Man Who Shot Liberty Valance** (1962) and **The Searchers** (1956). He cites the idea of turning the wilderness into a garden. He also cites similarities in very different films such as idea of the journey to a better future. This theme occurs in the journey of the Mormons in **The Wagon Master** (1951), the protagonists longing to go to the USA in **How Green Was My Valley** (1941) (set in Wales) and **The Informer** (1935).

Wollen also suggests that the identification of narrative theories such as the binary theory posited by Claude Lévi-Strauss can be identified in the films of Howard Hawks. This director works with a systematic series of oppositions (**The Big Sleep** (1944), **To Have and Have Not** (1946) – even the title demonstrates opposition.

The problem with the structuralist method is that it is a very reductionist approach. Identify the director, the films and then reduce out of that content the recurring themes, images, storylines and ideas. Alfred Hitchcock, for instance, demonstrated a liking for spectacularly beautiful blondes, such that the cliché the 'Hitchcock blonde' has become a definition for chic and a method of identifying a creative process that Hitchcock employed. Perhaps more appropriate identifying elements of Hitchcock as an auteur would be his preoccupation with all kinds of thriller, with the idea of female victimhood and, of course, more appropriate evidence of Hitchcock as auteur is his use of the camera to signify danger (the high angle rat-in-the-trap shot, for example).

Once proposed, the idea of the auteur became a matter for substantial discussion. Throughout the following decades, the French (through '*Cahiers du Cinema*'), the Americans, through the work and comment of Andrew Sarris, and the British through contributions to the journal '*Movie*' discussed and developed the idea of auteur theory in slightly different ways. Sarris particularly emphasised the style and personality of the director themselves. He suggests that the constraints of the industry on the director create a positive tension between the director and the industry rather than the industry itself hindering this process. He emphasises the personality of the director as an artist. He states that it is not so much what the director shows but *how it is shown*. This leads some theorists to identify the director as an auteur by studying mise-en-scène. This, in itself, counters the reductionist approach that preoccupies itself with structure and story rather than style.

In his chapter *Auteurs* in his book 'Adventures in the Screen Trade', William Goldman devotes a few words to deconstructing the concept and suggesting that it damaged Hitchcock's later work. He claimed that no director he had ever met would admit to believing in auteur theory but 'God knows what's silently eating way at them in the dark nights of their soul.'[28] However, he also states that he suspects that auteur theory would be with us for a while yet; he wrote that in 1983.

William Goldman may well be hostile to auteur theory because he, himself, is an author and screenwriter, not a director. He quite rightly states that the author writes the story, or the screenplay. The screenplay is then taken by a group of people, camera person, actors, editor, composer, producer, set designer, costume designer and, of course, the director.

NOTES:

27. Peter Wollen, *Signs and Meaning in The Cinema* (London, Secker & Warburg, 1967).

28. William Goldman, *Adventures in the Screen Trade* (London, MacDonald Books, 1983).

Bryan Singer: An Unusual Auteur?

Kenneth Turan (in 'Sundance to Sarajevo') points out that France is the home of auteur theory; that it 'deifies' the director at the expense of the other creatives on the set. He suggests that this might be the reason for the occasionally narrow interpretation of a good film that sets aside the commercial impulse in favour of the experimental, especially if that experiment is clearly originated by the director.

William Goldman argues that this is a construct that ignores the contribution of so many others. His case in point is that of *Jaws*. *Jaws* is a film that is often publicised as 'Steven Spielberg's *Jaws*'; but, says Goldman, Peter Benchley was the man who read a short newspaper article about a huge shark captured off Long Island and who then asked himself the question that so many novelists asks – 'what if?' He wrote the novel; John Williams wrote perhaps the most famous film theme apart from the Bond theme; Bill Butler was the cinematographer; Bob Mattey came out of retirement to build the shark; and Richard Dreyfuss, Roy Scheider and Robert Shaw all contributed great performances. All these people made the film *Jaws* the exciting classic it still is today. Goldman argues that auteur theory is simply a convenient economy of words that media (in the form of critics and marketing) has perpetuated from the French theory in order to save having to refer to all the contributors to any movie.

What Goldman points out, in his iconoclastic way, is that film-making is team work, a point that is made to students all the time when embarking on their coursework. Goldman might suggest that the only way to be an auteur is to write, direct and maybe even act in your film, a tall order, although some do it. In practice it is possible. Goldman subscribes more to a theory defined as metteur-en-scène. This theory defines the director as a highly competent mediator, someone who can put together all the elements in a film so that they represent all the contributions made as a cohesive whole.

Auteur theory, then, according to Sarris is about a discernible style that can be traced through a director's body of work, in spite of the variety of stories or genres that that director may choose to pursue. Metteur theory reflects more directly the ideas of William Goldman that the director pieces together a variety of contributions, including, if not especially, the screenplay in order to represent a film as a complete piece.

The question is – is Bryan Singer an auteur?

If you look on the internet encyclopaedia Wikipedia under auteurs, you will not yet find him listed. One of the main issues against him is that he was still very young (only 27) when he filmed *The Usual Suspects*. His list of films since then is still limited, and they cross genre in a way that auteur purists suggest should not occur. However, Steven Spielberg is cited as an auteur, having directed everything from sci-fi (*ET, Jurassic Park*) through human interest thrillers (*Jaws*) to war films (*Saving Private Ryan* (1998)). Bryan Singer has directed a neo-noir thriller and a set of superhero films: the probable definition of an auteur nowadays has more to with the ability to recognise a style.

If the definition of an auteur is in the uniqueness of style then what makes *The Usual Suspects* a film that might indicate the birth of an auteur? Repeated through this text and through the comments by actors and colleagues on the film is that Bryan Singer was very clear on what he wanted, particularly the visual style. Kevin Spacey stated that he was not a director who shot things arbitrarily in the hope of putting everything together in editing. He knew exactly what he wanted, each shot was planned and the representation of it through the cinematography of Newton Thomas Sigel allowed the film to represent itself to an audience almost exactly as Bryan Singer had seen it in his head. William Goldman clearly makes the point that the making of a film is a group effort and no one person can take responsibility for the final product (responsibility being the appropriate epithet, it is not always credit).

NOTES:

Bryan Singer: An Unusual Auteur?

Arguments for and against Bryan Singer as a metteur-en-scène:

For	Against
Ensemble cast – as stated above an ensemble cast is precisely the type of cast that provides a director with different elements to mould together as a representative whole.	The ability to mould a group of disparate elements into one cohesive style of representation may well indicate the mind and talent of an auteur.
Bryan Singer himself credits John Ottman with some powerful editing decisions, including the use of the 'blooper' footage of the line up which was not ever intended by Singer to be utilised in this way.	The clear vision that Singer brought to the film allowed colleagues to work within his vision, without it necessarily being their own.
The film was very clearly a combination of talents. Christopher MacQuarrie and Bryan Singer had known each other from school. John Ottman joined them at college. They were a team on the film.	Gabriel Byrne states that every bit of technique and every skill and understanding that Singer had was brought to bear on the film and that made it a Singer film.

Arguments for and against Bryan Singer as auteur are as follows:

For	Against
A preoccupation with overwhelming evil. The tagline to his film *Apt Pupil* (1998) was 'If you don't believe in the existence of evil you have a lot to learn'.	The structuralist approach to auteur theory would suggest that storyline, rather than a theme, is an important part of identifying a director as an auteur.
An ultimately evil bad guy. Since Keyser Soze his films have had comic book sources each involving exaggerated antagonists.	Again as a tool in identifying a director's personal interests this works, but is it an indication that the director is an original artist? It is not an original preoccupation.
Use of light, clarity and noir: Kevin Spacey describes how impressed he was by the clarity of *The Usual Suspects*. It is easy to forget that the film contains not only aspects of standard neo noir, but moments of great light and clarity. Similarly *Apt Pupil* and the snowy landscapes of the *X-Men*.	Sarris states that style is strong identifying element in the classification of a director as an auteur. There is no doubt that *The Usual Suspects* is tremendously stylish (see Chapter 2 on the semiotics of *The Usual Suspects*) but is this style carried on in Singer's other films, perhaps in the *X-Men*?
Bryan Singer seems expert at working with groups of actors (ensembles) and drawing out equivalent and original performances without the use of one A-list star.	Working with ensemble casts might actually indicate that Singer is more of a metteur-en-scène. Working with an ensemble requires precisely the skills of a director able to work in a team and build a film out of different elements

Is Bryan Singer an auteur? His youth and small body of work so far makes it difficult to state categorically one way or another. In recent years his work has been preoccupied with the representation of comic book heroes. Perhaps in the end those ideas will define him as an auteur and not *The Usual Suspects*. What remains true is that *The Usual Suspects* was truly an original film and the fact that it may never be repeated may well militate against the suggestion that Bryan Singer is an auteur.

NOTES:

Bibliography

Books

Bettelheim, B., *The Uses of Enchantment: The Meaning and Importance of Fairytales*, London: Penguin, 1991.

Branston,G. and Stafford, R. (eds) *The Media Student's Book*, London: Routledge, 2002.

Caughie, J., *Theories of Authorship: A Reader*, London: Routledge, BFI Reader, 1981.

Goldman, W., *Adventures in the Screen Trade*, London: MacDonald Books, 1983.

Hirsch F., *Film Noir: The Dark Side of the Screen*, New York: Da Capo Press, 1981.

Larsen,E., *The Usual Suspects,* London: BFI Modern Classics, BFI Publishing, 2002.

Lasswell, H D., 'The structure and Function of Communication in Society', in **L. Bryson** (ed.) *The Communication of Ideas*, New York: Cooper Square Publishers, 1964.

Monaco,J., *How To Read a Film: Movies, Media, Multimedia* (3rd edn), Oxford: Oxford University Press, 2000.

Points, J., *Studying American Beauty*, Leighton Buzzard: Auteur, 2003.

Porfino, R., Siver, A. and Ursini, J., *Film Noir Reader 3,* New York: Limelight, 2001.

Straczynski, M., *The Complete Book of Scriptwriting*, London: Titan, 1987.

Todorov, T., *The Poetics of Prose* (trans. from the French by Richard Howard; with a new foreword by Jonathan Culler), Oxford: Blackwell, 1977.

Turan, K., *Sundance to Sarajevo: Film Festivals and the World They Made*, Berkeley: University of California, 2003.

Voytilla, S., *Myths and the Movies: Discovering the Mythic Structure of 50 Unforgettable Films*, Michigan, Sheridan Books 1999.

Internet

www.hitchcock.nl/quo.htm

www.nbrmp.org/awards

Robert Weston, Article, Detour (1946) www.filmonthly.com/Noir/Articles/Detour/htm

www.imdb.com *The Usual Suspects* – Trivia.

Dr. Mary Klages, Associate Professor of English, University of Colorado at Boulder, *Claude Lévi-strauss: The Structural Study of Myth and Other Structuralist Ideas*, www.colorado.edu/English/engl2010mk/levistrauss.2001.htm

Yair Oppenhem, *The Functions in Film Music*, www.filmscoremonthly.com/features/functions.asp

www.moviesunlimited.com/truffaut/htm

www.johnottman.com

www.filmmusicsociety.org

www.filmsound.org

www.raindance.co.uk

www.launchingfilms.com

http://institute.sundance.org

www.boxofficemojo.com

www.imagesjournal.com/infocus/filmnoir.htm

Documentary

Nothing is What it Seems: The Making of *The Usual Suspects*, Prod. Louis Heaton, Channel Four, 1998.

Monitor BBC, 1962. 'Close Up On Hitchcock' also in BBC 1997 Prod. Nick Freand Jones.

DVD *The Usual Suspects* Special Features MGM, 1995.